SONGLINES

The Power and Promise

MARGO NEALE
& LYNNE KELLY

Thames &Hudson | national museum australia

First edition published in Australia in 2020
by Thames & Hudson Australia Pty Ltd
11 Central Boulevard, Portside Business Park
Port Melbourne, Victoria 3207
ABN: 72 004 751 964

First published in the United Kingdom in 2023
By Thames & Hudson Ltd
181a High Holborn
London WC1V 7QX

This edition first published in 2023

26 25 24 23   5 4 3 2 1

Thames & Hudson Australia wishes to acknowledge that Aboriginal and Torres Strait Islander
people are the first storytellers of this nation and the traditional custodians of the land on which
we live and work. We acknowledge their continuing culture and pay respect to Elders past,
present and future.

Thames & Hudson Australia thanks Professor Lynette Russell AM, ARC Kathleen Fitzpatrick
Laureate Fellow, Monash Indigenous Studies Centre, for providing editorial advice.

ISBN 978-1-760-76392-3 (paperback)
ISBN 978-1-760-76138-7 (ebook)

A catalogue record for this
book is available from the
National Library of Australia

British Library Cataloguing-in-Publication Data
A catalogue record for this book is available from the British Library

Every effort has been made to trace accurate ownership of copyrighted text and visual materials used
in this book. Errors or omissions will be corrected in subsequent editions, provided notification is
sent to the publisher.

This project has been assisted by the Australian Government through
the Australia Council, its arts funding and advisory body.

Front cover: Detail of Aboriginal art from St. Mungo Museum of Religious Life & Art, Glasgow,
UK. (CC BY-SA 2.0)

Series editor: Margo Neale   Typesetting: Megan Ellis
Cover design: Nada Backovic   Printed by Printforce UK

MIX
From responsible
sources
FSC® C109576

FSC® is dedicated to the promotion of responsible forest management
worldwide. This book is made of material from FSC®-certified forests
and other controlled sources.

Be the first to know about our new releases, exclusive content and author events by visiting
thamesandhudson.com.au | **thamesandhudson.com**

Praise for *Songlines* ...

'*Songlines* is one of those rare, thrilling books that can expand the mind in every direction.'
—Fiona Capp, *The Age*

'*Songlines* is a testament to the complexity, resilience and adaptability of First Nations cultures. It reminds readers that Indigenous peoples are and have long been scholars and intellectuals, a status historically denied to them by the depredations of colonial Australia. Indigenous expertise about Country is, Neale and Kelly demonstrate, a living knowledge with direct relevance to our shared present and future. As settler Australia confronts the damage it has wrought within a mere 250 years, we would do well to listen and learn from the knowledges that came before. Justice and healing will take different ways of knowing. *Songlines* is an important step in that direction.'
—Judges' report, Victorian Premier's Literary Awards shortlist for Non-Fiction

'... a model, a blueprint, for understanding and integrating traditional modes of learning and remembering into our own lives. ... It is a beautiful book with a beautiful message: respect ancient traditions and you'll discover not an outmoded, primitive way of life but a highly sophisticated technology. An unparalleled way of embodying and integrating knowledge and wisdom. And ensuring their survival for future generations.'
—Will Yeoman, *The West Australian*

'... one of the most important books any Australian might ever read, if we are to claim the right to our identity as Australians, rooted in this land and its history.'
—Barbara Lepani, Wild Mountain Collective

'With its use of personal story, history, art and even neuroscience, *Songlines* generously invites the reader to expand their consciousness with memory practices that are older than the Western Bible.'
—Chris Saliba, *Books+Publishing*

For Marandu Max Ivy Neale,
Ivy Sarah Tiernan,
Alinta, Solomon, Eamon and Minka

For Damian Kelly

NOTE ON SPELLING

Readers may note that for different language groups, variant spellings occur for similar words, cultural groups or names. This book presents word forms, object titles, cultural affiliations and names as advised by the communities and individuals involved in the National Museum of Australia's *Songlines* exhibition and research project.

COMMONLY USED TERMS

inma
ceremony or ceremonial song and dance

Tjukurpa / Tjukurrpa / Jukurrpa
the Dreaming

Kungkarangkalpa / Kungkarrangkalpa / Minyipuru
the Seven Sisters

pujiman
traditional times and life

Wati Nyiru / Yurla
the male Ancestral Being who pursues the Seven Sisters

CONTENTS

THE SEVEN SISTERS SONGLINE

All civilisations have epic sagas to explain the creation of the earth and transmit cultural values. The Seven Sisters Songline is one of Australia's most significant foundation stories.

It tells of an Ancestral Being in the form of a man, who wrongfully pursues seven sisters to possess them. To lure them to him, he shapeshifts into water, shade and various delectable foods, which the women need to survive in the desert. In this way, the story relays information that is critical for survival on this continent.

The many encounters the sisters have with their relentless pursuer result in the creation of the country, the evidence of which is recorded in the features of the landscape. They travel in an easterly direction across the continent, from a place near Roebourne in the west, sometimes disappearing beneath the earth before leaping into the night sky, always leaving a tracery of sites of significance.

It is a tale of tragedy and comedy, obsession and trickery, desire and loss, solidarity and sorrow that touches on life's moral dimensions: how to live with each other on this earth in a sustainable way; how to care for each other and share resources equitably. It also instructs on gender relations, kinship, marriage rules and other codes of behaviour. These lessons are embodied in compelling tales of intrigue, drama and passion that connect people and places across time. In this way, the story has been easily remembered and willingly retold to each generation for millennia. It is a saga of mythological dimensions and meanings.

FIRST KNOWLEDGES

MARGO NEALE, SERIES EDITOR

Everything starts and ends with Country in the Aboriginal worldview. Yet there are no endings in this worldview, nor are there any beginnings. Time and place are infinite and everywhere. Everything is part of a continuum, an endless flow of life and ideas emanating from Country, which some refer to as the Dreaming.

In the Dreaming, as in Country, there is no separation between the animate and inanimate. Everything is living – people, animals, plants, earth, water and air. We speak of Sea, Land and Sky Country. Creator ancestors created the Country and its interface, the Dreaming. In turn, Dreaming speaks for Country, which holds the law and knowledge. Country has Dreaming. Country is Dreaming.

It is this oneness of all things that explains how and why Aboriginal knowledges belong to an integrated system of learning that you will encounter throughout this series, starting here with *Songlines: The Power and Promise*.

Songlines, related to Dreamings or Dreaming tracks, connect sites of knowledge embodied in the features of the land. It is along these routes that people travelled to learn from Country.

Country holds information, innovations, stories and secrets – from medicine, engineering, ecology and astronomy to social mores on how to live, and social organisation, including moiety division and kinship systems. It is the wellspring from which all knowledge originates and gives rise to the expression 'Our history is written in the land'. By 'history' we mean all knowledge: sciences, humanities and ancestral knowledge, not only what is compartmentalised as Western history. If Country holds all knowledge, then Country is clever – thus the title of the National Museum of Australia's Clever Country online films, produced by Alison Page and Nik Lachajczak, which complements the First Knowledges books.

These aim to give readers an in-depth understanding of Indigenous expertise in six areas: Songlines; architecture, engineering and design; land management and future farms; healing, medicine and plants; astronomy; and innovation and technology. The authors of each book are pioneers in their respective fields and are working with these knowledges through a contemporary, not a historical, lens. As our knowledge system encompasses a concept of time that talks of 'the enduring present' and 'eternal time', the Western divisions of past, present and future, or historical and contemporary, are not particularly relevant, though they are useful at times. This recycling of time is embodied in the expression 'When you look behind you, you see the future in your footprints'.

To date, little accessible material, if any, has been available on Indigenous knowledges for general readers. We hope this series fills that gap. Furthermore, these books will introduce the knowledges of First Australians in ways that are in line with Indigenous ways of knowing and being, and overturn outdated ways of representing – or misrepresenting – Aboriginal and Torres Strait Islander peoples.

Some prevailing assumptions about our culture will be challenged and discussed in this series, such as: that Aboriginal people were only hunters and gatherers, not farmers; that fire is destructive, not a tool for managing the land; that we did not build houses and had no technology, no knowledge system and no history, only myths and legends; that we had no scientists, doctors or lawyers; that we were incapable of innovation. The view of the colonisers that persists is that we did not change. In truth, we have a long history as innovators and peoples who adapted to phenomenal climatic changes, including an ice age and rapid sea-level rise, pestilence and colonisation – and we are still here.

Songlines: The Power and Promise is the first book in this series because Songlines are foundational to our being – to what we know, how we know it and when we know it. They are our knowledge system, our library, our archive from which all subjects are derived. Today, in the digital era, this knowledge is accessed in multiple ways.

My co-author, Lynne Kelly, deepens and expands the Songlines concept in her chapters by explaining how the neural pathways of humans are engaged, and she connects our Songlines learning with other ancient cultures of the world. She explores the value to non-Indigenous people of understanding how the Songlines work as a system for the retention and transmission of knowledge to enhance their own lives.

Aboriginal culture was traditionally non-text based, so voice was the major means of communication, primarily through song and storytelling. We hear reference to voice in contemporary political terms, as in the voice to parliament through the Uluru Statement from the Heart or the voice for constitutional reform. We subscribe to the concept of the 'right to speak': that is, who is authorised to speak for particular areas of knowledge, which derives from who has the right to speak for Country. This relates to rights to and responsibility for specific stories or knowledge assigned through status and family lineage. For example, only some people have the right to speak for certain areas of Country, as you see at Welcomes to Country.

In this book, and throughout this series, we acknowledge the expertise of knowledge holders from both Aboriginal and Western disciplines. This form of co-design or co-authorship in practice is in the spirit of reconciliation, working well together interculturally. I write from an Indigenous perspective on my areas of responsibility to Aboriginal culture and knowledge in the museum context, and Lynne writes from a Western perspective on her area of expertise in memory systems. We are seniors in our respective fields and committed to Australia's shared history. Therefore, the tone and style of my writing is different from Lynne's, as it should be. There have been no attempts to homogenise our voices as might be the case in other co-authored publications; our cultural and individual differences are one of the strengths of this book.

While it is well known that colonialism has had an enormous impact on Indigenous societies, this book reveals the other side of that coin: the significant influences that Aboriginal and Torres Strait Islander cultures have had on Australian society and history, and the enormous contribution they are making, which, in many ways, mainstream Australia is only beginning to recognise. As co-authors,

Lynne and I consider ourselves fortunate to be in a position to provide some insights into the traditional knowledges of the First Australians, for all Australians.

The English language can't effectively describe the many new ideas you will encounter in this First Knowledges series, but we hope the concepts in these books will excite and provoke you to learn and expand your worldview to encompass limitless other possibilities, including ways in which you can learn from the Aboriginal archive of knowledge embodied in Country. In combination with the Western archive, this knowledge creates a third archive, available to all.

1

PERSONAL PERSPECTIVES

LYNNE KELLY

Why, oh why was I taught nothing at school about Aboriginal intellectual achievements? Why was I taught nothing about memorising my lessons using song, story, dance and bringing to life the landscape all around me?

I am mortified to have to admit that for much of my life I knew almost nothing about this country's First Nations cultures. Like most of my generation, educated in the 1950s and 60s, I had the impression that Indigenous people were fairly 'primitive', with superstitious beliefs and no understanding of science. What little we were taught was about how the British 'discovered' Australia and brought civilisation to our hot, dry shores. It was mentioned in passing that there had been Aboriginal people here, but my impression involved black men holding spears, and little more. It is horrifying to think of the proportion of Australians who emerged from our education system as ignorant as I was.

It was only when I started researching animal behaviour for a science book on crocodiles that I realised that Indigenous stories were not simple folklore but encoded accurate information about the local species. And I understood this after only reading the public stories, the equivalent of children's tales in Western society.

It finally dawned on me: Aboriginal people would not have survived if they had lived in a fog of superstition and non-scientific thinking.

I started finding Aboriginal science everywhere. It wasn't just the big animals like crocodiles and kangaroos that the people could identify and tell you a vast amount of detail about their habits. They knew all the birds, numbering in the hundreds. Most people I know could barely name a dozen of the most common birds, and this would be considered incredibly ignorant within an Aboriginal culture. Then I found studies of Indigenous knowledge of the hundreds of insects and other invertebrates in their environments. Add in hundreds of plants, unbelievable distances for travel, land management, genealogies, astronomy, legal systems, ethical expectations ... The list, I found, goes on and on.

My thinking became dominated by a single question: how the hell do they remember so much stuff?

That was how I stumbled on the fact that Indigenous cultures have memory skills that I desperately needed. I have a pathetically bad natural memory. At school, subjects like history and legal studies were very difficult for me, while foreign languages were nigh on impossible. I tried three different languages at school and again as an adult, studying for long hours, but my brain simply wouldn't retain the vocabulary. So I stuck to the subjects I could do using logic: mathematics, physics and computing.

I started my PhD research when I was in my fifties, looking at Indigenous knowledge of animals. In one of our first meetings, my supervisor, Professor Susan Martin, suggested that I investigate 'orality' and read Walter J Ong on the topic. Having never heard the term, I wrote down 'morality', wondering if I had already broken with some kind of doctoral etiquette. I discovered that Ong, author of the influential book *Orality and Literacy*,[1] was talking about the use of song, story, dance and a raft of other techniques to make information memorable by cultures in the world that did not use a written script. It was my first baby step to understanding how First Nations people could remember so much stuff.

But what Ong and other orality researchers did not tell me about was the land. There was no mention of Dreamings or Songlines.

Having encountered very few Aboriginal people where I lived in southern Victoria, it was a revealing moment early in my research when I met an elder at the Koorie Heritage Trust in Melbourne. He told me that the key to his way of knowing was his Country, and that singing the names of sacred sites along the Songlines created in his mind a set of subheadings to the entire knowledge base of his culture, a place for knowing about every animal, plant and person. He could sing his Songlines even when away from Country because he could move through the space in his imagination. His Country was always part of him.

I was very excited by this concept, and even more so when I tried to set up my own Songline and found that, suddenly, I could remember things.

My first experiment was to memorise the countries of the world. I found a list of them in population order and placed the most populous, China, just inside the entrance to my study, imagining a Chinese meal being delivered. Then I placed India at the bookshelf (a full Bollywood production going on underneath) and the USA at my desk, with a rather frightening image of President Donald Trump taking over my chair. Around the house and garden I went, astounded at how easily I could add a few countries each day. After 120 countries, I ventured out into my street. Circling a few blocks, allocating a country to each house, shop and side street, I soon had more than 200 countries and independent protectorates firmly in place.

Once I had hooks for the countries literally grounded in my landscape, I wanted to know more about each country and the relationships between them. Just as Aboriginal people have done with their Songlines for millennia, I started to build complexity on the firmly grounded structure. I started creating Songlines for all of prehistory and history, finding myself noticing details in my surroundings that had been simply background before. I became emotionally engaged with my landscape. I was starting to get a tiny glimpse of what Aboriginal people had tried to explain to me. I added characters whenever they belonged in the history pathway.

My neighbourhood became alive with people from the past and their stories: Einstein and Homer, Jane Austen and Joan of Arc.

Even if I don't engage with them every time I walk around my house and garden or through the streets, they are always there, rooted in the memory locations or travelling with me. In my imagination, or in the physicality of my neighbourhood, I can walk through every space on earth, through every country and across every continent and ocean. I can walk through time from the incomprehensible past to the inconceivable future. I now have somewhere to put every person, every country, every event, all the towns and lakes, oceans and rivers, every book and war, every human triumph and failing. My Songlines seem infinite already. My landscape has come to life; it is no longer passive. I can't stop asking questions. Was King John of England aware of the incredible culture at Great Zimbabwe or of the Ancestral Pueblo, both flourishing during his reign? Why did I know so little about Bangladesh when its population is so much larger than that of Russia, Japan, Germany or England?

I started to discover that there were the equivalent of Songlines all over the world: Native American pilgrimage trails, Pacific Islander ceremonial roads and ancient Inca ceques.

As I gained more insight into the way Songlines work, even at this superficial level, the more horrified I became about the past. If I was becoming so engrossed in my landscape after only a year or two of experimenting, how intense must it be for people who have lived their entire lives this way, as did their parents and grandparents, as have their forebears and ancestors for all of time? How traumatic must it have been to witness invaders build fences across Country and shoot anyone who tried to visit their sacred sites? The physical cruelty must have been horribly exacerbated by the intellectual deprivation. When Native Americans were marched off their lands into reservations, they called it 'the walk of tears'.

I started experimenting with the other memory devices I was learning about from Indigenous people. I was glimpsing the way in which art in many forms is integral to knowledge systems, and I began to copy them. I chose to copy the *lukasa* of the West African Luba people, even though I struggled to believe that a piece of carved wood with beads and shells attached could act as the effective memory device described in the research. These memory boards are miniature landscapes; the pathways through them are miniature Songlines. They have counterparts in every Indigenous culture, most profoundly in the art of Australia's First Nations.

Unlike the Luba memory experts with their long-established designs, I just grabbed a piece of wood and attached beads willy-nilly. I decided then to encode a field guide to the birds of my state, numbering over 400. Each bead became a family; I sang the families. Each family has a story attached, giving me all the species in it and information about them. The birds morphed into humans and back into birds again, depending on where the story took me. There's a long story for the thirty-six types of honeyeater, but very short stories for those with only one species. Despite my slapdash approach, my lukasa worked a treat. A second lukasa, which I designed more carefully and based more accurately on the Luba examples, was much easier to encode.

12

My Songlines, songs, stories, memory boards and artworks all meld seamlessly into a system that is far more complicated to describe than it is to use. My brain just jumps to the song or image it needs at any given moment. At first I could not explain the system to friends when they asked about it: it was too much like hypertext and too little like the linear flow of a book. I could only explain small portions at a time, demonstrating or giving examples, and now understand why it is almost impossible for Indigenous peoples to explain their knowledge systems. One Mutthi Mutthi man said it is too hard to explain from within the complexity of what you know so well. He asked me: 'How would you explain your knowledge system? Ours is so different that we don't have the right words in English.'

I gained a profound insight into this different way of thinking from Native American Pueblo writer Alfonso Ortiz and his colleague Richard I Ford, a botanist and anthropologist. From their work I learnt that in contrast to the yellow corn familiar to Western diets, Pueblo corn comes in a variety of colours, from almost black to white, and each type succeeds in different climatic conditions. Corn cross-pollinates very easily, and Pueblo farmers have for centuries – if not a great deal longer – planted their different colours in combinations. They plant each colour in a separate field, with the fields scattered and bordered by other crops as a buffer. They plant in a way that ensures nearby colours ripen at different times so as to reduce cross-pollination. All of this serves to reduce the high risk of total loss and the consequent starvation that could occur if they planted a yellow corn monoculture.

Ford writes about the Pueblo rules for seed selection and guides for planting in a Western scientific way, while Ortiz relates the stories of the Corn Mothers and Corn Maidens who encode the knowledge of corn. I fully understood Ford's explanation, but the Pueblo way of thinking was so unfamiliar to me when I first read about it that I struggled to see the connection to survival. Ortiz recommends that his readers read Ford's work as complementary to his own. Ford explains that whether informed by agricultural science or Pueblo mythology, the outcome is the same: rigorous management of corn varieties enables survival in a harsh and unpredictable climate. Both archives encode the same information, just using very different storage formats.

The neuroscience of our brains is the common factor that led cultures all over the world, and throughout time, to create memory devices that brought their landscapes to life and ensured that they would not lose the knowledge essential to survive both physically and culturally. We know that mnemonic devices were universally used by cultures who were heavily dependent on their memories for survival. Wouldn't the same be true for cultures who are no longer here to explain their knowledge to us, such as those who built the ancient but enigmatic monuments that still stand around the world, with no one left to tell their stories?

I visited Stonehenge. How would Neolithic people have preserved their Songlines as they gradually settled in one place and farmed? The pattern at Stonehenge was similar to the thousands of other stone and timber circles across the UK, Western Europe and North America, and as far as Easter Island. The materials used reflected those available in the local environment and the decorated objects indicated independent cultures, but the underlying structures were remarkably similar. I was able to find clear archaeological evidence for ancient knowledge spaces, with constant reference to the landscape. It seemed clear that these cultures had represented their Songlines and sacred places locally with standing stones and decorated posts, astronomical alignments and decorated objects. They had created essential public and restricted performance spaces in every case. Archaeologists study the Neolithic monuments built by oral cultures only 5000 years ago. Why haven't they asked for advice from Aboriginal elders whose oral cultures date back at least 65,000 years?

I completed my PhD and wrote a few books. But readers kept asking me the question I so keenly wanted to avoid: how could these techniques be used to learn a foreign language? I had to face the demons that had haunted me since my schooldays.

I took on French. I created Songlines and sacred sites, sang songs and engaged with characters, created stories. I was learning in a different way – vivid, visual and emotional – and gained much insight and pleasure from the process. Then I became really ambitious and decided to learn Mandarin. French and Mandarin are so different that I had to adapt my methods, but underneath there were still Songlines and songs, stories and dance, and a world full of characters.

Everything I was learning started to mesh together. The geography and history and art of China integrated with the language I was learning. The birds became part of the environment, not separate entities. I could see that everything had a place and was named and could be known. I understood that for Aboriginal people, Country was a network of knowledge on a grand scale, and was amazed that throughout my life I had never been exposed to something so powerful.

Non-Indigenous observers report their surprise at the emotional response displayed when the place names from a Songline are sung, but I am no longer surprised about this. When I list the locations of one of my Songlines, my world is full of characters, images, funny or sad or frightening stories, and a precious store of knowledge. I sing my songs in the shower. I sing when I am cooking or gardening. Loud and clear, I sing my knowledge. My Songlines are now so familiar that I feel a strong emotional attachment to them. They are home. I could not have understood this had I not tried it myself.

I was shocked then to find that I was still not experiencing even a fraction of the power of Songlines. I travelled to Canberra in early 2018 to see the National Museum of Australia's exhibition *Songlines: Tracking the Seven Sisters*, curated by Senior Indigenous Curator Margo Neale in collaboration with a community curatorium. The exhibition took me on a journey through the desert lands of many Australian Aboriginal cultures, including those of the Martu, Pitjantjatjara and Yankunytjatjara peoples. The stories were told and sung and danced. They were bawdy, emotional, frightening and humorous, stacked with adventure and tension. They were everything a good narrative should be. For that reason, the knowledge they contain has remained memorable for millennia, and will continue for as long as the stories are told and performed.

The Indigenous storytellers in the exhibition told their ancient narratives using multimedia, enabling me to hear exactly how Indigenous voices express their Songlines. I saw some of the most evocative art I have ever seen; pictures in books could not move me as these artworks did. But the most revealing experience was under a huge dome, where visitors could lie down and be taken by Aboriginal voices through Country, an ever-changing landscape. Becoming immersed in this 'third archive', I realised I still had a very long way to go to fully experience even my comparatively small Songlines. I went back to the museum three times to enter this world, and it became less alien with each visit.

My world now is much richer than it was before. I have lost none of the love I have for books and technology, but now I have a swag of new tools to learn in a different way. The pragmatic and the mythological, the utilitarian and the emotional, the Indigenous and the Western all meld into a wonderful complex whole. Now that I have experienced this third archive, I will never stop learning.

MARGO NEALE

Like Lynne, I could ask why, oh why was I not taught about my people at school? And furthermore, when I was, why was I taught such a limited and demeaning version?

The truth is probably that this is all the dominant culture itself knew about us, and they had no desire to know more – if indeed they believed there *was* more. After all, if there was more, there was no point knowing about it as our extinction was imminent.

Aboriginal people, viewed as remnants of a bygone age, were studied by a handful of academics and some enthusiasts motivated by a 'salvage' mentality to save what remained of the culture before it disappeared. Of course, in our school years we didn't know about the massacres, the strychnine-laced flour, the Black Wars, the taking of children, our freedom fighters and the protests. All of this bears some comparison to the general German public claiming ignorance of the Holocaust. It was the job of the missionaries to give us a dose of Christianity and 'smooth the pillow of a dying race', granting Aboriginal people a passport to the afterlife. Little did they know that we had already taken care of all that eons before Christianity, and with passports that never expired or got withdrawn.

We were viewed as a culture without civilisation, with no books and no history – only myths and legends to amuse and entertain us around the fire at night. The new arrivals to this continent could not see that we had a complex religion and spirituality, that our 'voodoo-type' objects were sacred artefacts and our weapons were tools for hunting food sustainably. Perhaps it's just as well they didn't know this, as they may have seen our material culture as competition to the Bible, and destroyed it.

The colonisers thought we had no houses and no clothes and were just vagrant wanderers. Such opinions were likely influenced by explorer William Dampier's 1697 book, *A New Voyage Round the World*, and his observation that 'The inhabitants of this country are the miserabilist [*sic*] people in the world.'[2] Lieutenant James Cook offered a counterview, writing in his journal: 'they may appear to some to be the most wretched people upon Earth, but in reality they are far more happier than we Europeans; being wholly [*sic*] unacquainted not only with the superfluous but the necessary conveniencies [*sic*] so much sought after in Europe, they are happy in not knowing the use of them.'[3] He went on to comment on the people's tranquillity, equality and lack of need for material possessions, such as houses and clothes, acknowledging that the country provides for all.

In 1902, a member of the Tasmanian parliament dismissed the need to include Indigenous people in the national census on the basis that 'There is no scientific evidence that he [*sic*] is a human being at all.'[4] It is not surprising that this demeaning view of Aboriginal people persisted so strongly when you consider that only a century ago, the hugely influential Sigmund Freud wrote of Indigenous Australians as 'the most backward and miserable of savages'.[5]

We were called the 'Aboriginal problem', and interest in our society and culture was pretty well confined to finding further justification for our removal. This included taking our children away, thus stealing our future and hastening our apparent demise. Many white people fervently believed that they were giving these children a chance of a better life in this brave new world – a white-only world reflected in the 'White Australia policy'.

When I was growing up in the 1950s and 60s, my schooling was very much skewed to the Western educational system.[6] The society I lived among, outside my family, was not Aboriginal. Like many, if not most, of us living in the towns and cities of the urbanised south-east, I was certainly not schooled in the knowledge stored in Country, although I learnt about it later. I grew up in a small country town in Victoria with no visibly Aboriginal people around. In contrast, people who grew up at the nearby missions of Lake Tyers and Ramahyuck, where I learnt later that I had relatives, experienced a collective Aboriginal identity. They had been trucked into these depots of assimilation since the 1860s from their Countries further afield. Though most were no longer living on Country or being immersed in the master archive stored in Country, it would be a mistake to believe that there was no learning of culture going on. The resident elders always had Country in mind and transferred knowledge covertly. Language and practising culture were forbidden, but fortunately an embodied knowledge system such as ours does not need books or a human-made classroom to be taught.

The authoritarian regime Aboriginal people were living under and their treatment as second-class people, without equal civil rights, created a great reluctance in many parents and others to burden their kids with their Aboriginality, which they feared would disadvantage them severely, as it had done them. When we asked our elders questions about our respective pasts, we would invariably be fobbed off with 'You don't need to know' or 'I don't know'.

My mother married 'out', as they say, to a Royal Australian Air Force man and moved to the RAAF base far from family. In hindsight, I was learning bits and pieces of remnant Aboriginal culture from my family – mainly my grandmother on her visits, often with the aunties – but it was covert. My grandmother loved trips to the bush, and around the billy we would hear stories and songs of birds, animals and totems, studded with unusual words, and of her desire to go back to Country. Her Country sounded like a fantastical place belonging to another world, yet we were sitting on it. As kids in the pre-television era we were immersed in Enid Blyton's Secret Seven and Famous Five books, and comics featuring Superman and the Phantom with their hidden 'other' identities, so I found this shroud of secrecy around our Aboriginality mysterious and enticing.

At home there was a strict code of 'Don't talk to the neighbours'. Visitors were discouraged for a range of what seemed acceptable reasons at the time, and there were certainly no sleepovers in our house. I thought all of this was normal. Occasionally my 'hail-fellow-well-met' father, of Irish descent and disposition, in defiance of my mother's objections, would bring home his raucous drinking mates from the pub after closing time, and Mum, in fear, would lock us girls away. But I thought those gatherings were hilarious. The Aboriginal and Irish mix was 'deadly', both genetically and socially. We had a lot in common: both oppressed peoples and both fringe dwellers of the British Empire with a larrikin humour that was a key tool in our survival kit.

The 1950s and 60s was a period of assimilation, where children were being removed or separated, as my mother was, or 'missionised' or placed on reserves. The strategy of survival devised by Aboriginal people living in mostly white suburbs, if they thought they could get away with it, was to 'pass as white' – in public at least. This was not an uncommon practice in an era when governments were attempting to 'breed them out' – the thinking was that if you breed the black skin out, you would solve the Aboriginal problem as there would be fewer black people around. This hope was predicated on the belief that our culture was only skin deep. Looking white and being trained to be white was considered to be the answer to the Aboriginal problem. Later, many of those armed with a Western education and with lighter skin, who'd been targeted for removal, became activists for Aboriginal rights.

When you could not pass as white, a 'dusky' complexion or other giveaway features were explained away by being of Polynesian descent or another heritage that was more acceptable to mainstream Australia than Aboriginal. When our great-uncles visited, their dark skin colour was said to be because they came from the west and worked outdoors in the strong sun. There was always a feasible explanation. This and other attempts at concealment were a common story among many of our mob up until the 1980s. My grandmother, near the end of her life in the mid-1960s, burnt her birth certificate, thinking that by doing so, she could hide her past and protect her family from discrimination and removal. Her best friend, Pearl, was heard to say over my grandmother's grave, 'Don't worry, dear friend, your secret will die with you.' Though Grandma knew our ancestry was held in the family as a closely guarded secret, she naively believed that erasing the official proof with the strike of a match and a promise was the ultimate protection she could afford us.

Sally Morgan's book *My Place*, published in 1987, cut through the shame and stain of this legacy of colonialism that resonated for so many of us, permitting a kind of 'coming out'. Sally's mother's and grandmother's denial of their Aboriginal heritage and desire to remain silent, and her search to find her people, had parallels with the stories of Aboriginal families like ours who were living in the parts of Australia that had borne the brunt of colonisation.

Sally suffered criticism from both sides of the cultural divide for exposing what she had discovered about the attempts at erasure of Aboriginal identity and other brutalities.

The 1980s was an era of reclamation that reached a climax around the 1988 bicentennial year, when Aboriginal people marched in protest bearing banners saying 'We have survived' and 'We have nothing to celebrate'. The surge of pride in our culture that was displayed, combined with anger at the injustices, united us in a struggle that fuelled a movement not only to reclaim our culture but also to redefine our identity. With the dissipation of fear, the children and grandchildren of previous generations became free to identify with their Aboriginal ancestry as a source of strength, not vulnerability, and began to unravel the secrets of their pasts. It is an ongoing process that can both unite and divide families.

Mind you, there are those of a right-wing disposition in the media who continue to have great difficulty with Aboriginal identity being anything other than what it was pre-invasion. As Bundjulang artist Bronwyn Bancroft, who for a time was told she was of Polynesian ancestry, wrote on the label accompanying her 1991 painting *You don't even look Aboriginal*: 'For years we were punished for being too black and now we are punished for not being black enough.'[7]

I had many conversations about the complexities of Aboriginality in the wake of the mission era with Yorta Yorta artist and countryman Lin Onus (1948–1996), who believed until the early 1990s that he was Wiradjuri. Even though he grew up an only child with his well-known enterprising Aboriginal father, Bill Onus, and his Glaswegian mother, Mary McLintock Kelly, in middle-class Melbourne, he suffered. 'All my life I have struggled with my whiteness and my Kooriness,' he said.

Surrounded by the trappings and culture of white society while connected to his father's community at Cummeragunja, Lin wasn't totally comfortable with his Aboriginality in some parts of his early life. His parents clearly wanted to give him what they believed was a better chance than his Aboriginal peers and cousins would have. He was dressed in sailor suits, learnt music, lived in a house with paintings by Eugene von Guérard and was regaled with stories about his grandfather on his Scottish side, who built a coach for the Queen of England. Ironies abounded.

Lin's father had married out, as did the mother of another late, great artist, Gordon Bennett (1955–2014). Gordon was raised among white society by his Aboriginal mother and Anglo-Celtic migrant father, and only learnt about his Aboriginal heritage as a teenager. He was caught in the generation where his parents passed him off as white to protect him from the discrimination and indignities his mother had endured as a 'dormitory girl' at Cherbourg mission in south-east Queensland and later as a domestic worker. Gordon recalled entering the workforce as a teenager and 'really learn[ing] how low the general opinion of Aboriginal people was'. His response to such prejudice was 'silence, self-loathing and denial of my heritage'.[8] All he knew about Aboriginal people and culture he had learnt at school, absorbing the racist attitudes vividly evident in his painting *The Coming of the Light* (1987), which features English alphabet blocks with A, B, C and D, and racial slurs such as abo, boong, coon and darkie.

Somehow, at primary school, the term 'abo' escaped me as being racist. I thought it was my nickname because of my spindly legs and, in the days before everyone wore a hat and sunscreen, my easily tanned skin, my darker complexion. I didn't know I should be offended as I didn't know where the word was coming from. The time I do recall being offended – deeply offended – and think about often to this day was when I was caught mouthing a penny and a teacher yelped, 'Don't do that – you don't know where it has been! A dirty Aborigine could have touched it!' Or words to that effect.

Talk about living in a bubble. In my home in the 50s we had no television, books or magazines, and no conversations about what I should think of being of Aboriginal descent or of Aboriginal people more broadly. There were no other Aboriginal kids at school, so I felt special and different. But I knew not to talk about it. It was my little secret. Yet I loved playing the Aboriginal girl in all the games, building mia-mias or 'humpies', as Aboriginal shelters were referred to then. I stood on one leg, gathered food, ground seeds, made damper (sort of), painted up and organised others to perform ceremony with me. It wasn't until years later that, along with my extended Gumbaynggirr family, I started attending New Year's Day smoking ceremonies on Country, employing many of the elements I had 'rehearsed' innocently as a child and later saw in cultural practice in Arnhem Land. I have since become the unrivalled damper queen of my clan!

From the pictures in my primary school texts and the cartoon strips *Saltbush Bill* and *Witchetty's Tribe*, I had the view that Aboriginal people were different, exotic and adventurous. They lived exciting lives in deserts, on islands and in the bush, and their kids didn't have to go to school. They never lived in towns – they were far too special for that, in my child's view. Town was ordinary. Once, an Aboriginal family came to live in a tent down at the creek where we played, and I was very envious. What fun to be able to camp all the time beside a creek, go fishing and cook on an open fire! I knew nothing then of the circumstances behind why this family were itinerant and fringe-dwelling on the creek. Later, in high school, I got it – to my shame.

Aboriginal people were not officially counted in the national census until 1971. (Ironically, the landmark 1967 referendum that changed this situation was only successful because more than 90 per cent of mainstream Australia, particularly the churches, supported it in a way no other referendum had been supported.) Rather, it was as though we were regarded as flora or fauna[9] and thus had some 'native appeal' and unusual behavioural habits worth recording, as one would of animals in the wild. This is what we saw in our school textbooks.

I was eighteen when the 1967 referendum was held. I went to teachers college in the big city of Melbourne and jumped at my first opportunity, in 1968, to go to the desert on a trainee-teacher excursion. Most of the other students went to the Whitsundays or other more 'normal' places, but this is what I had been waiting for: to meet the desert people I had seen in picture books, to go somewhere to feel the pulse of Country with language, ceremony and the Dreaming, which outsiders then called the Dreamtime (the term Songlines did not appear for another twenty years). Although it didn't mean much out of context, I walked the 'Dreamtime' tracks, learnt about the totems my grandmother had spoken of, the possum and the cockatoo. I visited sites and caves with the old people, sat around fires and felt the throb of the chant-like songs and clap sticks whistling through the night air and the ground vibrating beneath the feet of the dancers. It was a more raw, 'authentic' experience than many of the well-packaged, over-rehearsed cultural tours of today. Communication with community people was not a problem: their English was as good as mine, if not better. Most of them had been at Hermannsburg mission, where they were the beneficiaries of a bilingual education.

While climbing a hill one day with young Aboriginal guides, I remember singing the rousing gospel song 'We Shall Overcome', popularised by American folk singer and activist Pete Seeger. The Northern Territory was gearing up for the land rights movement which culminated in the NT *Aboriginal Land Rights Act 1976*. Something stirred deep inside me. I wanted to know more, to feel more, to reconnect with an Aboriginal past to complement my contemporary urban life. I was looking to extend my education to include the classical, just as Italian Australians might go to Italy to round out their education. Many urban Aboriginal people, including artists Trevor Nickolls and Lin Onus, did this in the 1970s and 80s. Lin referred to his annual visits to Arnhem Land as pilgrimages.

To complete my education this way was clearly not possible under the education system of the time (it still isn't), but there was no going back now. Within two years I was on the old Ghan train heading for Alice Springs, then on a plane to Darwin and a charter to Milingimbi Island – it took four or five days all up. This was during the last vestiges of the assimilationist era (1951–62). Located in the Crocodile Island group in Arnhem Land, close to the mainland, Milingimbi was a Methodist and then a Uniting Church mission. The mission era was sighing its last breath, and my husband, Bruce, and I (we were married in December 1970) were sent there as teachers by the NT Welfare Department because it could no longer find enough missionaries to staff its schools.

On our first day at Milingimbi in January 1971, I was asked by schoolchildren, 'Are you a teacher or a Christian?' Up until then they had only experienced missionaries, and with this dribble of new people called teachers coming into their world, people who looked and behaved quite differently from the missionaries and who mixed with them, they had to extend their category of outsiders to not one type of person but two. We were only the second non-missionaries to arrive in this insular place that had been largely closed to the outside world for nearly fifty years – though it had been occupied in various ways for tens of thousands of years by the Yolŋu people.

I recall missionaries standing on soapboxes in the Milingimbi camps on Sunday mornings, threatening hellfire and damnation, then later slipping into our donga for a closeted drink behind drawn curtains. These last dregs from the mission world were not of the calibre of those driven, committed people of earlier years. They thought they had the local Aboriginal people Christianised but didn't realise that the real attraction to church on Sundays for many was the ceremony and ritual, the singing, the red cordial, bikkies and cups of tea. These missionaries were not kidding anyone, least of all the locals. Those who did become committed Christians invariably got hurt. I recall a local Aboriginal pastor getting excommunicated when cultural values clashed. Under Aboriginal law he was obliged to take on the wife and children of his deceased brother to look after, but he was seen as a bigamist in the eyes of the church and removed. He was devastated.

The missionaries gave me a wide berth. I was subversive in a number of ways, such as socialising with the local 'blacks', having them in our house and other dastardly deeds. I got immersed, and not just in the mud of the mangrove swamps where I went crabbing with the women and learnt their Gupapuyŋu culture and lore. Painted up, bare-breasted and dancing in ceremonies before it became popular among latter-day outsiders, I learnt language and was initiated into the Bangadidjang skin group and given the name Burria. The name you were given defined your relationship to your skin group and related groups, which determined your roles and responsibilities and ensured a cross-cultural exchange of goods, skills and knowledge.

It was in Milingimbi that I first appreciated what connectivity meant in traditional Aboriginal society, particularly in relation to the kinship system, where everything and everyone is related and connected to everything else. This system is simultaneously rigid in structure and flexible and accommodating of change. Peggy Anderson Napurula, originally from Papunya in the Western Desert, had married Milingimbi man James Gurrwangu, a local Gupapuyŋu man whom she had met at Kormilda College, a post-primary residential school in Darwin for Aboriginal students. This union was highly unusual, as the moiety system then strictly determined marriages with the relevant skin groups within the same language group; marrying for love was not condoned.

When Bruce and I visited Peggy and James' camp for the first time, Bruce, learning that Peggy was Warlpiri, introduced himself by his skin name, Juburula, thus making him her brother. She had acquired a Gupapuyŋu skin name as James' wife, since his wife's skin group is pre-ordained. This is where the rules can be made flexible under certain circumstances that I would not be privy to. Bruce, being Peggy's brother, automatically had the Gupapuyŋu equivalent skin name of Warmud; I, being Bruce's wife, could only be Bangadidjang, one of a limited number of skin groups. We instantly had a relationship not only with Peggy's extended family but with the whole group, including groups beyond Milingimbi. I became sister to James' sister Gapany and later, cousin to actor David Gulpilil's father and grandfather. Wherever we went from that time forward – Yirrkala, Canberra or even Beijing, where I was with some Yolŋu people recently – I could establish a relationship simply by introducing myself by my skin name. This would lead to other people and relationships. The bonds created through this classificatory system can be stronger than blood. Children are often brought up by classificatory uncles, aunties, mothers and fathers who are not necessarily their direct biological relatives.

This network of connectivity continued when we moved to Maningrida, a government settlement for Aboriginal people on the Arnhem Land mainland, some 73 kilometres from Milingimbi. We were related to everyone, even whitefellas who were given a skin group. David Gulpilil was an occasional student in my class at Maningrida and we had a skin group relationship through his Uncle Jack Mirritji, a Djinang man. My husband's parents were embraced as family when they visited Gulpilil in Sydney years after we left Maningrida. He was so happy to see them and, although he had never met them before, wept tears of joy as he considered them to be actual family. He felt connected as they were the parents of his uncle and aunty – that is, Bruce and me. Through this encounter he experienced a connectivity to Milingimbi, to Mirritji, to his uncle and so on. It is this kind of connectivity between people and place, past and present, and concomitant roles and responsibilities that is alive in the Songlines, a bit like when you start talking to a person you have never met before and find out that you are both from some obscure town and went to the same school decades ago. There is an instant relationship.

At Maningrida I experienced another example of the kinship system at work in daily life. While driving with Djinang man Don Gundinga on a seriously corrugated road at a fairly rapid rate, which people do in an effort to skim over the tops of the corrugations, we spotted a man walking beside the road. The walker acknowledged us with a quick flick of the hand. In that instant he communicated who he was, his skin group and his language group, and thus his relationship to Gundinga. It turned out he was Gundinga's grandfather/grandson, which meant he was related to both Bruce and me. (Gundinga was Bruce's grandfather by the classification system, though he was the same age; he can also be the grandson in this system.) This led to a whole lot of other connectivities.

Bruce and I were part of the Outstation Movement, as it was known in the 1970s (it is now referred to as the Homeland Movement), where the government of the day assisted Aboriginal people to return to Country after removals in previous decades. We needed facilities to service schools we'd erected out of bush materials or tents up the waterways and along the coast, so Bruce and another teacher went to Darwin to secure two boats. There were no roads to Maningrida then, so they had to go there by sea. Accompanying them was Charlie Mulumbuk, who had travelled the route some years earlier when he worked on the barges. The barges were huge and had navigational and radio equipment, but the dinky boats Bruce was using were ill-equipped for the open sea, particularly the stretch off the Arnhem Land coast. Everything that could fall off the boats fell off before he and his colleagues left Darwin Harbour – the awnings, the windscreen and other bits and bobs. They hugged the coastline as closely as they safely could for the first day, but when night fell, the seas heaved and crashed and visibility was completely gone. With clouds obscuring the stars, and the deafening sound of the agitated sea, Charlie would stare out into the inky vastness and after some computing in his head would point and say definitively and repeatedly, 'That way.' Not once was he wrong. It would have been dire if he was. The boats continued over two nights and by the third day, the assembled and much relieved Maningridians lining the shore spotted two small dots on the horizon and welcomed the battered boats and bruised bodies of the intrepid travellers.

How they did not perish at sea remains a mystery. Charlie couldn't tell us how he knew – he just knew. Was he sniffing the air for land smells, working out the direction of wind, feeling the waves beneath his feet and the roll of the boat? The answer, as always, lies in the Songlines, knowledge of which allowed Aboriginal people to navigate not only vast amounts of information efficiently but also vast distances. I have no doubt that this story has entered the Songlines for future recounting. The Songlines, or Dreamings, are like a big sponge that keeps on absorbing new stuff and releasing it with a little pressure.

Jumping ahead a few decades, and with multiple books and exhibitions in the field of Aboriginal art, culture and history behind me, I came to understand that although I had local experience, I did not know how this knowledge was connected more broadly. I had a visceral connection and commitment to all things Aboriginal, but it wasn't until I started on the Songlines preservation project in 2011 that I realised I was missing the glue, the matrix that tied it all together. Putting together the exhibition *Songlines: Tracking the Seven Sisters* as lead curator with a community curatorium really clinched it for me. I then had to find a way of explaining the Songlines to your average museum punter while not dumbing down or undermining the substance and sophistication of the system.

If the Songlines as an integrated knowledge system is an embodied one, it needed to be transmitted experientially via linked sites on Country, at least virtually. Three deserts were therefore mapped across the gallery and Songlines were drawn onto plinths like wayfinders that visitors to the exhibition could follow. The paintings became portals to places where the knowledge was primarily stored, ready for activation by the participant 'travellers' – as I called the visitors to the exhibition. The elders appeared on life-size screens at strategic sites to authorise each traveller's journey and assist in the embodiment of the story.

And it worked.

After reading Lynne Kelly's book *The Memory Code*,[10] I invited her and others, some of whom will write other books in the First Knowledges series, to an Indigenous Knowledges roundtable at the museum. This was the icing on the cake. Lynne added the missing ingredients to the matrix. While I had experienced Songlines-in-action on the ground, learning about neural pathways and the global scale of mnemonic systems was mind-blowing. It was the original World Wide Web. However, the more I learn, the more I realise I don't know.

2

EVERYTHING STARTS AND FINISHES WITH COUNTRY

Why do most Australians know so little about the deep history of this continent they call home? The late Paddy Roe, an elder from the Kimberley region in the far north of Western Australia, challenges us with his profound observation: 'You people try and dig little bit more deep – you bin digging only white soil.'[1]

What is generally taught in schools and universities is the country's history of only the past 200 years or so, which in some ways is not surprising and in other ways is very surprising. If history is told by the victors, we should not have been shocked to hear prime minister John Howard assure all Australians in 1996 that they should feel 'comfortable and relaxed' about their past. He meant it was okay to ignore the tragic aspects of our history: 'It's very important that we don't, as a nation, spend our lives apologising for the past.'[2]

Aboriginal and Torres Strait Islander history has been relegated to the footnotes. Now, in this new era of 'truth-telling', some rectification is underway. The establishment of Reconciliation Australia in 2001, the apology to the stolen generations by prime minister Kevin Rudd in 2008, the formation of the Prime Minister's Indigenous Advisory Council by Tony Abbott in 2013, and the newly established advisory group on developing a First Nations 'voice' to parliament are examples of this. This latest initiative was preceded by other attempts at having conversations across the country for constitutional reform, such as the now defunct 'Recognise' campaign (2012).

As a person of Aboriginal and Irish descent, I too was taught the history of the colonisers and subjected to a convenient and stereotypical view of Aboriginal people as primitive natives on the verge of extinction, without possessions and exhibiting no desire for material advancement. This, in combination with the greater sin of Aboriginal people making no apparent productive use of the land, provided all the justification necessary for the colonisers to forcibly relieve my ancestors of their land and their sovereign rights.

This view about land use has rightly been challenged by both Aboriginal and non-Aboriginal people. The works of historian Bill Gammage and Aboriginal author Bruce Pascoe have arguably had the most impact here. Gammage's book *The Biggest Estate on Earth: How Aborigines Made Australia* (2011) convincingly shows that Aboriginal people did farm the land, but in a different way from the colonisers. Here were 'farmers without fences'. Aboriginal people had devised sophisticated, sustainable methods for hunting and gathering through working with nature and harnessing its rhythms. Using their deep understanding of Country, they worked lightly with the land.

Pascoe's powerful and controversial book *Dark Emu* (2014) and its influential precursor by Rupert Gerritsen, *Australia and the Origins of Agriculture* (2008), refute the notion that Aboriginal people made no productive use of the land. Gerritsen and Pascoe show in different ways how Aboriginal people employed sophisticated methods for working with Country for food production, housing construction and clothing. Their methods were sustainable and not in conflict with the environment, and so were not visible to the colonisers, who could only see improvements that controlled nature, not harnessed it. The settlers' buildings stood in contradiction to the land, and their multiple layers of clothing, headwear, footwear and handwear alienated them from the environment and climate.

The irony is that these books on Aboriginal methods of sustainable living draw on observations recorded in the diaries of early colonial explorers and settlers. Such descriptions were perhaps an inconvenient truth for the colonial powers of the day, who most likely viewed Aboriginal achievements as 'simple', primitive or uncivilised, and the people as incapable of 'sophistication'. These early firsthand accounts had been written out of subsequent histories, until now.

To paraphrase the French poet and novelist Victor Hugo: 'There is one thing stronger than all the armies in the world, and that is an idea whose time has come.' These recent books have shaken the established view of Australia's First Nations people and are timely against the current backdrop of climate change, destruction of the land, rampant fires and a pandemic; they are getting purchase that would not have been possible ten years earlier. Authorities are only now beginning to realise that Aboriginal people knew how to manage the land sustainably, having done so for millennia. Other related traditional knowledges that sustained life in Australia are also inviting a closer look. How much of this knowledge is now retrievable for practical purposes is the question – but the principles hold.

So why aren't Indigenous knowledges taught in schools? The resurgence of self-determination and our right to manage how we are represented, which we refer to as Indigenous agency, is a worldwide movement. Over the past two or three decades we have increasingly demanded a voice in all things that affect us, particularly all things Indigenous. Such a development has caused many educators to feel nervous about teaching Indigenous subjects, which they feel should be done by Indigenous people. While that might be ideal, a few realities must be taken into account.

Firstly, there are few of us. As our agency increases, so does the demand for our cultural knowledge, protocols and understandings. Welcomes to Country, for example, are increasingly standard practice for all manner of events. A large proportion of our willing and able population are occupied by this work, as well as by cultural awareness workshops, seminars on Indigenous knowledges, oral histories, language courses, and committee and community work. We are spread thin.

Secondly, our tertiary-educated people tend to go into the housing and health sectors – not to mention sport and the arts, where we punch well above our weight. According to the Australian Bureau of Statistics, in the 2016 census we accounted for some 2.8 per cent (649,200) of the Australian population, and 53.1 per cent of us were under 25 years of age, 22.2 per cent were over 45, and 4.8 per cent were over 65.[3] This leaves few able or available to become secondary school teachers.

Then there is the issue of under which discipline Aboriginal knowledges should be taught. Though the Western education system would categorise and teach Indigenous knowledge as 'history', our knowledge system is more than that: it is integrated, not compartmentalised into disciplines. The Aboriginal view is that history is culture and that it can't be separated or relegated to one subject alone. For example, knowledge on Country, for the tens of thousands of years prior to British arrival, integrated the humanities and sciences and encompassed the creation of the continent, ecology, astronomy, geology, arts, law and religion. We tell history differently on Country, as is shown by the Parnkupirti Creek story about two dingoes in Chapter 4. The term 'history' is interchangeable with the term 'story' (from which it derives), but story carries more weight in the Aboriginal world, as history does in the Western world.

We need to find ways to bring understanding of Indigenous knowledges into schools and to the general population despite hardships and sensitivities, or they will always remain secondary to the national story. It stands to reason that regardless of people's views or biases, the Aboriginal story is the foundation story of this continent and thus central to the Australian story. It has to be fully integrated into the Australian curriculum and viewed as mainstream, and it has to be taught by teachers, whether or not they are Indigenous. When the stories of Ned Kelly and Thunderbolt are taught, for example, so should the stories of Aboriginal freedom fighters Jandamarra and Pemulwuy, who also found themselves outside the law resisting what they believed were oppressive regimes. When teaching about the Eureka Stockade, Aboriginal protests such as the Tent Embassy and the Freedom Rides could be included along with other parallel historic moments. Similarly, teaching in the sciences could include Indigenous knowledges in the areas of ecology, geography, geology and astronomy. Why do we teach Japanese and Italian in schools as second languages, and not Aboriginal languages?

The ways of teaching the humanities and the sciences can only be enriched by Aboriginal ways of learning, in which story, contained in the Songlines, plays an active part. We need to move into a new space. We are all Australians – same but different, as us mob say.

One of the most educative and moving ways of teaching all Australians about the foundational history of this country is through the arts: visual art, music, performance and writing. Aboriginal ways of being and knowing have enhanced all of these disciplines, and can help make the arts more experiential, immersive and holistic, involving all the senses. An engaging example is the National Museum of Australia's landmark *Songlines* exhibition. Seven years in the making, it changed the way people saw themselves as Australians and their relationship with the First Australians, showing that we share not only a continent but also a history. Senior custodian Rene Kulitja, who spends her time moving around the world teaching the way Aboriginal people learn, saw her role in the exhibition as 'to learn those people up about Songlines'.[4] The exhibition and its messages captured world interest, and *Songlines* is destined for an international tour.

Professor Mick Dodson, an Aboriginal academic formerly at the Australian National University and now the Northern Territory's Treaty Commissioner, said the exhibition was like a communication portal, just as this book aims to be. *Songlines* was a virtual journey along the Songlines, mapped across 1000 square metres. The gallery became Country and visitors become travellers and initiates, learning as real initiates do, travelling the Songlines and being taught by elders who guided their journey. Paintings functioned as gateways to sites on Country that hold the knowledge, much like libraries. The geographical features of these sites act as a mnemonic system, which you can read more about in Chapter 3.

From the outset of the exhibition, the elders were very clear about why all Australians need to know about the Songlines. If you want to truly belong to this country, you have to know your story about this place, this continent and its creation. It was about teaching you *your* stories, not just sharing ours – otherwise, you won't take root and belong. As elder and senior spokesperson for the *Songlines* exhibition Inawintji Williamson said, 'This is your story too.'[5] This is a significant shift and was not missed by those who experienced the exhibition. According to feedback, more than 90 per cent of visitors felt invited and included and not like voyeurs ogling other people's culture as if it had nothing to do with them. They were learning about Australian culture and history – a culture that is fundamental to our shared history. The elders hoped that those who engaged with the exhibition would develop a sense of co-ownership and feel some responsibility to preserve the Songlines as part of Australia's natural and cultural heritage.

All Australians are the legatees of a continent with the deepest human occupancy in the world and arguably the longest continuing culture in the world – which doesn't mean unchanging. This is why Songlines are relevant not only to their traditional custodians but to all Australians.

This journey digs deeper than white soil. We travelled the Songlines in the tracks of the Seven Sisters across three deserts, amounting to some 7000 kilometres, with a relay of traditional custodians and knowledge holders passing the baton as the Songlines stretched beyond one language group's Country into the next. It is future-proofing the Songlines by ground-proofing them.

WHAT'S IN A NAME?

Across the country, Aboriginal and Torres Strait Islander peoples have adopted with alacrity the word 'Songlines' as a cross-cultural term for the concept of *Tjukurpa*, *Altyerre*, *Kujika* and other localised terms for Songlines or Dreamings – another introduced and equally well-received Western word. These terms are used interchangeably. There is no question in the minds of Aboriginal people across the country that they own these words.

As is commonly the case with cross-cultural terms and translations, the words are both useful and misleading. Anthropologist Philip Jones from the South Australian Museum, in his essay in the *Songlines* exhibition catalogue, warns of overly simplistic definitions of the terms. He reminds us that the word Songlines is a translation that attempts to define what is essentially undefinable: 'its meaning will always harbour ambivalence, imprecision and elusiveness'.[6] This is also the case with *Tjukurpa*, a language word used by Anangu people of the Central Desert that has been taken up in many areas of the continent with reference to the Dreamings or law/lore. It conceals as much as it reveals.[7] You can only get a sense of it through learning how it works on Country. If you ask an Aboriginal person, particularly from remote Australia, what Songlines means, they might look flummoxed and then say, 'It's the law' or 'It's the Dreaming'. No further explanation is necessary. It's like asking someone why they live.

In his essay in the *Songlines* catalogue, Professor Mike Smith, formerly of the National Museum of Australia, looks at the many possible functions of the term in the context of maps, parables and allegories, scripture and oral history. He concludes that perhaps the closest we can come to understanding it is as 'a framework for relating people to land, and to show that this relationship is inalienable or the law'.[8] Though it might exhibit functions that bear a resemblance to those Western categories operationally, it is an all-encompassing worldview where all parts are indivisible from all other parts and functions.

Songlines are becoming lost or fragmented in many areas of Australia due to people's extended absences from and loss of Country. The Yanyuwa people of the Gulf Country express this loss in terms of 'broken songs'. Anthropologist Deborah Bird Rose refers to it as 'wounded spaces',[9] while academic John Bradley calls them 'torn songs' in his book *Singing Saltwater Country*.[10] The Yanyuwa describe broken *Kujika* (Songlines) as still being in Country but having to be pulled up from Country and then put back into Country, or Country will close in. That is, once the song is activated by people's return to Country and by their singing the songs of Country, the song is deposited back into Country. The power of the song needs to be returned to Country to keep it alive, or Country will die – a bit like recharging batteries. In ceremonies witnessed in the Central Desert, the ceremonial ground is prepared with a painting relevant to the Dreaming ancestor being honoured, and the highly ritualised performance takes place on one day or over many days. The power of the performance is absorbed into the Country, and all remnants of the ground painting are erased so as not to lose any of the power – the power that goes into the earth and thus into the Songlines.

3

KNOWLEDGE IN COUNTRY AND THE THIRD ARCHIVE

Inuit man Dempsey Bob said, 'The trouble with whitefellas is that they keep all their brains in books.'[1] This simple but perceptive pronouncement invites us to ask, 'Where else can we keep our brains?' By brains, of course, Dempsey is essentially referring to knowledge. Where do we archive the knowledge of a culture for current and future generations if not in books, cloud computing and various electronic platforms?

A clue to the answer lies in those powerful words of Paddy Roe: to dig deeper, beyond the 'white soil'. Our history is written in the land – deep in the land – and transmitted via the Songlines. The deep history of this continent is in that black soil beneath the white soil. It lies in the millennia before white settlers starting laying down their stories only a couple of hundred years ago, a mere skin that tells nothing of the people who were here up to 65,000 years before them. It is the long human occupancy by a people who know how this land was created, why it looks the way it does, and why the animals, plants and insects were created and behave the way they do and what their purpose is.

Most significantly, this knowledge carried in the Songlines decrees that humans are equal with all things animate and inanimate. Together we form part of a web, in which each component sustains the land and keeps the archive alive. Every single thing has a place and a kinship with humans: the wind, the dirt, the rocks, and even shit: in Arnhem Land there is a Diarrhoea Dreaming. If it exists, it has a place. It is a fact of life, not a value judgement, so it does not need an explanation. But it does need a place to belong.

There is also little distinction between past and present. Macassan vessels called *praus*, which frequented our northern shores in search of trepang (sea cucumbers) from at least the 1700s and possibly earlier, and aeroplanes visible during the Japanese bombing of Darwin have found their place in the Dreaming. They appear in rock art and are still included in song cycles and Songlines and performed at ceremonies in Arnhem Land today.

For Dempsey, the idea that our knowledge comes primarily from humans rather than from the creator ancestors, and that it is deposited in something as disembodied and dislocated as a book, is difficult to understand, if not unfathomable. As a Pintupi man put it to anthropologist Fred Myers, the law 'is not our idea'.[2] Creation and the law laid down for all to follow comes from the creator ancestors.

In this master archive, humans are documents, archived according to kin, knowledge and ancestral relations to places. Writer and artist Kim Mahood, who had a long association with the Martu people of the Pilbara, noted that they know their Country so intimately they are part of its story. They don't need maps. This was the premise of the exhibition *We Don't Need a Map: A Martu Experience of the Western Desert* (2012–13). As Mahood said, 'They are the map, all of them custodians of the interlocking story that is Martu country.'[3]

Art historians Darren Jorgensen and Ian McLean observe that:

> The archive is a source of power. It takes control of the past, deciding which voices will be heard and which won't, how they will be heard and for what purposes. Indigenous archivists were at work well before the European Enlightenment arrived and began its own archiving. Sometimes at odds, other times not, these two ways of ordering the world have each learned from, and engaged with, the other. Colonialism has been a struggle over archives and its processes as much as anything else.[4]

Taking the land was also taking the archive, destroying our identity and raison d'être – not that the colonisers could have conceived of such an alien concept as an archive in the land. When they arrived on the Australian continent thinking they had discovered a terra nullius, they began documenting – measuring and mapping, naming and writing, and all the other ways in which they recorded their knowledge. They didn't realise that every centimetre of the continent had already been mapped and archived.

Many Aboriginal families, particularly those like mine who were deeply affected by colonisation, had long interrogated both the Western archive and what remained of our Indigenous master archive to retrieve what we could of our stolen pasts. The Indigenous impetus to assimilate aspects of Western archival processes into their own master archive is a natural part of the contemporary circumstances of Indigenous cultures in the wake of colonisation. A good early example is the establishment in 1971 of a Western-style museum in the community of Yuendumu, 290 kilometres north-west of Alice Springs along the Tanami Road. The initiative came from Yuendumu's Darby Jampijinpa Ross after he worked with his group's collections at the South Australian Museum in the mid-1960s and realised how such a keeping place could protect secret sacred objects that held the knowledge. The purpose of the Men's Museum, as it was called, was to house sacred material and stories that had been dispersed in secret caves across Warlpiri territory where the custodians used to live. From the mid-1940s to the 1960s, the custodians had been relocated by the government to the settlement of Yuendumu, and their material culture needed rehousing. If the people's lifestyle changed to a more sedentary one, then so too must the means of keeping the knowledge be adjusted: custodians need to maintain a connection to their sacred objects to keep the objects alive.

It is this capacity of Aboriginal people to adapt to change that has enabled their survival for millennia. These objects are portals to the places where the knowledge resides in Country, and thus Country can be accessed through them via song and performance, even from a distance. They are not *about* Country: they *are* Country.

Museums of today have taken account of Indigenous archives in varying ways, especially museums that have recently been established or that have built new sections on Indigenous knowledges, such as the National Museum of Australia, the Melbourne Museum and the Western Australian Museum. Over the past two decades in particular, Indigenous staff and Indigenous communities have mentored the collections for which they have responsibility or to which they have connection, and communities have been continually reconnected to these collections. It is now common practice for museums to allocate a special section of their collection to secret sacred objects. Like the archive on Country, the special section has restricted access and is governed by traditional practices according to gender, status and family lineage.

The interaction between the Indigenous and Western archives has unlimited possibilities, but only if each talks to the other. For example, many Aboriginal and Torres Strait Islander artists in the past twenty to thirty years have consulted the Western archive to reconnect with material held about their families and to regain some control over their past, in what Darren Jorgensen terms the 'archival turn' in contemporary art.[5] Urban-based artists have consulted their family histories in colonial archives, and interrogated others for information and misrepresentation. Among the first Aboriginal artists to do this was multimedia artist and photographer Leah King-Smith who, in her series *Patterns of Connection* (1991), retrieved colonial photos of Koori people from State Library Victoria's archives and reinserted them into an Aboriginal space. In the hands of an Aboriginal artist, these unknown people regained a place of dignity grounded in layers of history. The subjects recorded as unknown were given back an identity and reconnected virtually with Country. Other artists, such as Fiona Foley, Julie Gough and Brook Andrew, in their installation works, have challenged the colonial perception of our people as flora and fauna or mere objects of study. The deconstruction and reconstruction of the Western archive by Indigenous artist-activists become acts of cultural empowerment.

———

So, what is this archive held in Country, and how is it distinguishable from the Western archive? How does it work? How are the artists or cultural practitioners archivists? What is the relationship between the two archival systems, and how do we figure in the space between?

The master archive held in Country is an organic, living and breathing personage often referred to as 'our mother' by Aboriginal people. It is depicted in David Mowaljarlai's map *Bandaiyan, Corpus Australis* (the Body of Australia) and is crisscrossed with Songlines that Mowaljarlai calls 'landstories'. All Aboriginal people have a defined place in the family born of Mother Earth. Their identity is linked to place via their family lineage, their conception site and their birth site. With this identity come particular sets of knowledge eked out over time through age-grading rituals and accompanied by increasing levels of responsibility to maintain the received knowledge and the place where the knowledge resides. Lines of connection link individuals to each other and their respective Country through a sophisticated kinship system that traditionally involves a moiety

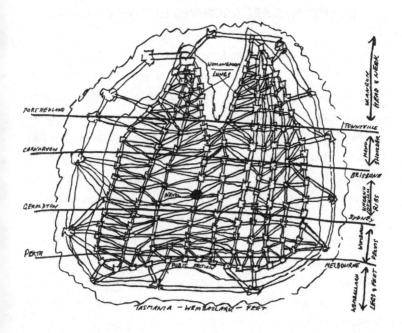

Bandaiyan, Corpus Australis (the Body of Australia)

system and skin groups. In different parts of Australia, particularly in the southern and eastern areas that bore the brunt of colonisation, this kinship system has evolved into different forms that are referred to by my family and others as kitchen-table kinship – that is, where aunties and uncles sitting around the kitchen table connect people through family names and determine their kin relationships, which are not always by blood. This form of kinship resonates with other clan-based groups.

SONGLINES ARE ARCHIVES HELD IN COUNTRY

Songlines, a term coined and popularised by English writer Bruce Chatwin in 1987,[6] refers to a knowledge system – a way of retaining and transmitting knowledge – that is archived or held in the land. They can be visualised as corridors or pathways of knowledge, like Dreaming tracks. The Songlines or Dreaming tracks are often associated with animals (such as a native cat or dingo), natural elements (such as Water Dreaming) or contemporary events (such as the Darwin cyclone of 1974 – the Dreaming provided an explanation for this phenomenon and ceremonies were created). They are also associated with major ancestral beings, such as those embodied in the Seven Sisters Songlines. Some Songlines are confined to small local areas, like Yam Dreaming or Bandicoot Dreaming, and others, like the Seven Sisters Songlines and Marlu the kangaroo, travel the entire continent.

As a set of complex arterial connections, the Songlines comprise an organic network of lines crisscrossing the continent along distributed nodes of concentrated knowledge, often referred to as sites of significance (places) and also known as story places. Like libraries, these sites contain stories in which knowledge is embedded. Some of the stories are open to all, but many are not: rather, there are many layers of the same story, each with varying levels of access. Stories are called 'open' or 'closed'. For example, the Seven Sisters Songline story in the National Museum of Australia's exhibition or in a book is an open story, which the custodians call the schoolkids' version. Beyond this version, the deeper layers of a closed story will only ever be known by a select few. At one level, access to knowledge is age-graded – similar in some ways to the system we progress through at school and university in the Western education system. Further access to deeper knowledge is not democratic but gendered, age-graded and continually negotiated.

A person's bona fides as an archivist are strictly based on family lineage, where the traditional owner, with custodial responsibilities to a place or site, becomes simultaneously carer or keeper, archivist, reader and contributor. While Western archivists also have to go through training, they need not have a familial relationship to an archive. In the Indigenous system, not all people can know all knowledge, and because it is a non-text-based system, you can only be told by the right people, at the right time, in the right place. Because you gain access through family lineage, it inherently becomes a subjective system and the custodians of the knowledge have a strong responsibility to keep it alive. In contrast, the Western system is more objective (except for some materials that are restricted for entirely different reasons) as it is managed by people employed to do the job, rather than by people born to the job.

In the Aboriginal archive at given sites, landforms tell the history of their making. A landslide of red rocks may tell of a bloody ancestral battle; the fissure in a rock face may be associated with the Seven Sisters and their journey to escape a lustful pursuer; and a monolithic rock at a cave opening may indicate the presence of the creator ancestor who made the cave. In this respect landforms are a type of writing, like ancestral scripts. They serve as a mnemonic rearticulated in 'open' or popular songs, dance and paintings.

As Yirrkala elders have expressed many times: Country cannot speak for itself, so art must speak for Country.

On another level, these sites are terminals to which only a few archivists have the password. The password gives them access to deeper, more secret or sacred histories, the story behind the story, which is often told in a language considered to be ancient and not accessible to others. These stories, whether they be open or closed, are portable versions of the master archive embedded in Country, over which we travel.

INDEXING COUNTRY

The use of songs to call up Country – 'singing up the land' – is perhaps the most ancient form of indexing. As Kim Mahood wrote:

> Story was patterned into songs that told the names of country, told when and where edible plants grew, where the marlu (kangaroo) and kipara (bush turkey) and parnajarrpa (sand goanna) lived, told of the grasslands and sand dunes and salt lakes and the ancestral beings who inhabited them. And water, always water. Yinta (permanent spring) and Jurna (soakwater) and Jila (snake entity) the life force of the desert.[7]

Songs were learnt 'as people travelled to the places named in the song and the rhythm of walking took the song into the body. Through the body, song became dance, which in turn became ceremony.'[8] Painted with the signs of the ancestral beings being sung,

54

the dancing body unlocked the knowledge of the master archive. The contemporary practice of painting on canvas derives from body painting and is an extension of such archival practices. It is geared to the sedentary lifestyle and capitalist economy of today. To this day, many remote-area Indigenous artists sing in a kind of chant as they paint. Indeed, many Western contemporary artists paint to music, as if fulfilling an ancient habit. As Anmatyerre artist Emily Kame Kngwarreye (c. 1910–1996) sang her brush across the canvas, she would raise her head and peer to a place beyond, in the direction of Alhalkere, her homeland, which was the source and subject of the song. Her primary Dreaming was Yam Dreaming, and it was not only her responsibility to ensure its survival at Alhalkere through both physical and spiritual maintenance but also her raison d'être. Kame, her middle name, means 'yam' in her language, and a hole in her nasal septum is where she would carry a yam seed as an embodiment of herself. She would cradle the seed in her palm and say, 'This is me.' At other times, in a rare visit to a gallery distant from Country, she would touch different parts of a painting and sing its particular verses.[9]

The power of song to access the Aboriginal archive underpins a project that Sue Davenport and Peter Johnson, founders of community organisation Kanyirninpa Jukurrpa (KJ), developed with the Martu people from the Pilbara region in Western Australia. Being familiar with both Western and Aboriginal ways of archiving country – that is, Western visual cartography and Aboriginal songs – the Martu provided a classic opportunity to 'text' the third archive. Through singing, Martu people located on a Western map inaccessible remote sites that they had either never visited or had not visited since they were children. Later, when their work was checked off with a satellite map, the degree of accuracy, cartographically speaking, was remarkable.

Singing Country can locate places previously unknown by the singer. When a Western person was driving in the area of the Canning Stock Route in 2012 with two local Aboriginal people aged in their late forties to early fifties, every ten minutes or so a land feature would cue a song from them. At one point, one of the men excitedly asked the driver to stop the car and indicated that over to the left side of the road there was a waterhole high on the other side of the escarpment. When asked how he knew this if he had not been there before, he said it was in the song his aunty had taught him. With some scepticism the driver agreed to walk several hundred metres and scale the rubbly escarpment. To his amazement the waterhole was exactly where the song stated it would be. This was no surprise to his informants – they would have been surprised if it *hadn't* been there.

THE THIRD ARCHIVE: THE SONGLINES PROJECT

How does the relationship between the Western and Aboriginal archives work? How and why did it emerge?

The cultural, political and economic imperatives driving this archival turn can be clearly seen in the efflorescence of Aboriginal art over the past two decades and the emergence of recent groundbreaking exhibitions like *Songlines: Tracking the Seven Sisters,* and the cultural heritage preservation project that preceded it, *Alive with the Dreaming! Songlines of the Western Desert*, as well as the *Yiwarra Kuju: The Canning Stock Route* exhibition with the 'Return to Country' project before it. In this process, the Canning Stock Route was reclaimed by its traditional custodians and reinscribed with its ancestral history and Songlines.

The Songlines cultural heritage preservation project *Alive with the Dreaming! Songlines of the Western Desert*, or the Songlines research project for short, was initiated by a large group of Anangu traditional owners in collaboration with the Australian National University and the National Museum of Australia. With a sense of urgency, Anangu elder Mr David Miller, chair of Ananguku Arts and Cultural Aboriginal Corporation, said at a meeting in Canberra in 2010, 'You mob gotta help us … these Songlines, they are all broken up now … you can help us put them all back together again.'[10]

This kind of entreaty had been heard many times in the preceding years by those working on the Anangu lands. Elders feared the loss of knowledge as a consequence of the younger generation being distracted by the technological wonders of the 21st century. 'They don't want to hang around with the Elders, they've got rap, hip-hop and smartphones,' said elder Lizzie Ellis. 'When the young people today are at that young stage, they don't realise the importance of their culture.' She said that only when they get older and are 'married up with kids' do they want to know their stories, their place and cultural responsibilities. But by then, the last of the elders who have the knowledge will be gone. Rather than despair, the elders were optimistic and proactive and figured that the Western system of holding knowledge was what they needed. They would digitise their Songlines and knowledge in the world the younger generation inhabited, and store it in the Aboriginal-managed archive Ara Irititja, meaning 'stories from a long time ago'.

Ara Irititja was set up to preserve cultural knowledge and record story, song and performance using various Western technologies. This epic intercultural and interdisciplinary research project integrated Indigenous and Western knowledge systems and pioneered a radically new approach to understanding and managing our shared cultural and natural environment. By tracking the Seven Sisters Songlines across three states and deserts in the Anangu Pitjantjatjara Yankunytjatjara (APY) Lands and Ngaanyatjarra and Martu lands, we could explore archaeological, ecological, visual and performative aspects of the Songlines in an integrated rather than a compartmentalised way – which is how these desert people know their Country.

The Indigenous communities initiated the project with an Aboriginal governance structure led by the elders according to the *Tjukurrpa* (Dreaming). After all, it is the Tjukurrpa that is the law that determines who can go where, with whom, when and why. It designates who has the right to speak for different parts of Country. So, instead of a project conceived wholly within a Western archival paradigm, the museum and university facilitated the communities to extend their archival framework using Western methods and new technologies, thus producing a hybrid research model. Collectively, Anangu and Western scholars, who were referred to as equal knowledge holders, combined their skills to track the Songlines ecologically, visually and performatively over some 7000 kilometres and 600,000 square kilometres. Through Aṟa Irititja, which I refer to as a third archive, the Songlines project brought the Western archive much closer to the Aboriginal master archive. Aṟa Irititja effectively delivers Aboriginal knowledge through a Western archival system.

The intention of the Songlines project, as it is for Aṟa Irititja and other Aboriginal community archives, is that future generations will access knowledge in the digital archive as a kind of repatriation exercise. This archive is culturally nuanced organisationally and operationally to accommodate such a translational role. While anthropologists and other researchers have deposited knowledge of Country and culture in the Western archive since colonisation, the typical Western archive is not geared to the repatriation of Indigenous knowledges. However, many Western archives are now heading towards this by incorporating Aboriginal agency in all directions and at multiple levels. This front-end process is enacted by Aboriginal people, for Aboriginal people, in an Aboriginal-managed archive, in contrast to the back-end variety of research motivated by the fear of Aboriginal people dying out that was conducted by Western researchers in the past. The 'salvage' mentality that motivated Western scholars, collectors and others from the 1900s to the 1980s to grab as much information and as many objects as they could before the Aboriginal race died out or became assimilated has been replaced in large part by consultation with Aboriginal knowledge holders, recognising a dynamic culture.

The intent of Western and Aboriginal archives is associated with the universal desire to maintain cultural integrity and transmit knowledge over generations. The third archive aims to combine the advantages of the Western archive, such as material preservation, with Indigenous people's own knowledge systems, while transcending the objectifying systems that underpin the modern Western archive.

With this in mind, Western and Aboriginal researchers, elders and others set about re-archiving the Seven Sisters Aboriginal archive into a hybrid Indigenous–Western format as part of the *Alive with the Dreaming!* project.

COUNTRY IN MIND

Going back to the question of the nature of the relationship between the two archival systems and how we figure in the space between requires us to look at a couple of different situations on the ground. The first is when non-Aboriginal artist John Wolseley, a serial collaborator with Aboriginal artists, was undertaking a project with Yolŋu artist Djambawa Marawili at Blue Mud Bay in north-east Arnhem Land. Wolseley described his realisation of the difference between his approach to Country and that of his collaborator:

> Since the early days of European settlement there has been a tradition of heavy-footed artists drawing and documenting parts of the continent about which they know little. As for myself, when I arrived at Baniyala I was just plainly discombobulated! Here I was with Yolngu artists … with such brilliant ways of expressing in paint their vast knowledge about the place.[11]

Wolseley felt he was starting from scratch, and that in the etchings he produced he 'may have found a way of making ignorance a virtue'. 'There I was', he says, 'on the edge of the sea with a blank unmarked etching plate and an empty mind.'[12] While Wolseley's interest was in the exquisite patterning, shape, hues and random placement of, for example, a mangrove leaf, for Djambawa, standing beside him, the leaf was a prompt for ancestral stories related to Baniyala.

Experiencing the empty mind – a starting point and desired condition for many non-Indigenous artists – is an impossibility for Aboriginal artists. As incarnations of ancestral beings, their minds are brimming with associative information. While Country is an archive of ancestral actions, the full extent of the archive can be accessed and worked only by the custodians with the knowledge and authority to do so. As with all archives, the archivist doesn't just guard the archive: they interpret and add to it, engaging creatively with it to keep it alive, or to keep its knowledge relevant and active in the present. For the Aboriginal archivist it is more than a job or even a passion, as one might see with Western archivists – instead, it is their life's purpose. They are effectively present-day incarnations of their archive.

The anthropologist Alan Rumsey described Aboriginal archiving as an inscriptive and interpretive practice through which 'Country' becomes 'story'.[13] In other words, the Aboriginal archivist – whom we often know as the artist or maker, both inadequate Western terms – activates the knowledge embedded in a site by carrying some part of that knowledge to the site and carrying away an enhanced experience of that knowledge. A kind of mutual knowledge transfer occurs between place, person and history.

A very different figuring in the space between the two archival systems is evident in the 2013 collaboration between Western filmmaker Lynette Wallworth with eight senior Martu women from the East Pilbara, which reveals a more immersive interaction of Western and Indigenous knowledge systems. This collectivist project was realised in a multimedia installation work called *Always Walking Country*, comprising time-lapse footage of the execution of an epic 3 metre × 5 metre painting titled *Yarrkalpa (Hunting Ground)*, from the first artist's stroke to the last. The footage was placed at the heart of the installation and flanked by two equally epic context films.

The eight senior knowledge holders painting the canvas were archiving knowledge for the young rangers charged with caring for their Country at Parnngurr, a community five hours' drive east of Newman. They were also doing a kind of backup to safeguard the knowledge in the third archive for future generations. This process of knowledge transfer enacted with paint on canvas may on the surface appear to be only a Western process, but on viewing the time-lapse footage of the ten-day painting process compressed into forty minutes, you are left in no doubt that what you are witnessing is ceremony on canvas. With the canvas laid flat and undercoated black,[14] each woman seats herself on the part of the canvas that cartographically approximates her Country in relation to the other custodians. The women eat, nap, drink and physically slide over the canvas, repositioning themselves for each subsequent part of the painting, while kids and dogs run across it. Most of us know that Aboriginal art from remote regions is painted flat, but through this experience of seeing the canvas being painted, we feel the breathing, living surface become Country. As Wallworth describes it in the *Songlines* catalogue: 'The painting calls everything around it into itself. When we travel back across country, I feel as though I am moving across the painting ... I started to see the painting as a skin lifted from the land, still holding something of the sinews of the country beneath it.'[15]

The content of this monumental painting is encyclopedic. It is a visual archive of knowledge held in Country and is read like a person reads Country. But in this format, which draws on Western as well as Indigenous knowledge systems and resides in a Western gallery, it becomes the third archive. The collaborative process that created it saw Western audiovisual technologies and the artistry of Wallworth combine with the Indigenous knowledge system via the agency of eight traditional custodians. This immersive sensory experience is a different kind of figuring in the intersection from that of the artist John Wolseley.

Layers of knowledge and intellectual processes are embodied in *Yarrkalpa (Hunting Ground)*, as described in the *Songlines* catalogue. There are individual stories and accounts of the *pujiman* days (bush days before the white man), the movement of the Seven Sisters and other ancestors across the landscape, and nuanced knowledge of plants and animals, seasons and fire, permanent water, ephemeral soaks and underground seepage. The depiction of a small patch of *tinjil* (white coolibah trees) in the upper right section of the painting indicates many things: that the ground is low-lying and waterlogged in the wet season, that it has grasslands favoured by bush turkeys, that it is a good place to dig for wild onions, that in winter the witchetty grubs will fatten in the trunks and branches. Every part of the painting is dense with information, either literal or implied. The south-west corner is Kumpaya Girgirba's rendition of *nyurnma* (freshly burnt country) for hunting *parnajarrpa*, the goanna that is a staple bush food and is caught in astonishing numbers when the conditions are right.

The painting records a world intimately known to these Martu women, showing the country around Parnngurr, where many of them live today – the playing oval, houses and roads. The Seven Sisters, or *Minyipuru* in Martu language, traverse the north-west area of the painting, from east of Parnngurr rock hole to the hill in the north, stalked by Yurla, as he is called in Martu language, and his restless desire. They are a part of the quotidian landscape, a manifestation of the omnipresent Jukurrpa, enmeshed with the activities of daily life. The south-east quadrant shows a vibrant patchwork of fire scars, the result of regular local burning that regulates and stimulates the growth of food plants. If you were to sit down with the painters and ask them to explain the burning practices, they would tell you that there are several distinct stages of burning and renewal. *Nyurnma* reveals the tracks and burrows of reptiles – especially when it is still covered with ash, seen as whitish patches on the canvas. *Nyurnma* includes the first growth of green shoots and is followed by *nyukura*, when plants mature and produce edible fruits and seeds. *Manguu* means the spinifex is ready to burn again, and *kunarka* is old-growth spinifex that will burn fiercely and cause hot-season bushfires if it is struck by lightning.[16]

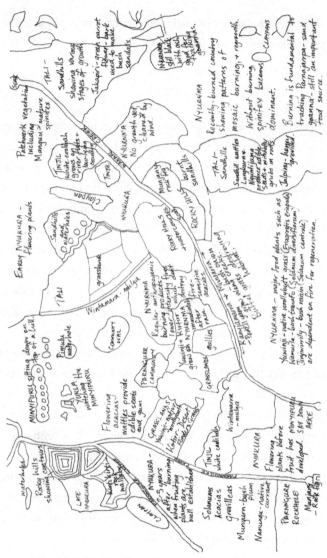

Diagram of *Yarrkalpa (Hunting Ground)*

Yarrkalpa (Hunting Ground) is epic in more than physical size: it is epic intellectually and ancestrally.

———

The prominence of the Indigenous archive in contemporary art brings a new perspective to knowledge held in Country. Thinking of Country as an archive endows a level of authority on Indigenous art that has not previously been acknowledged beyond, perhaps, the field of anthropology, and establishes new relationships with Western institutions such as museums, which think in archival terms.

In Australia there has been a discernible escalation over the past decade in the overt and intentional public use by Aboriginal people of both Aboriginal and Western archives, as evidenced in the proliferation of large-scale intercultural, multidisciplinary projects like the Songlines project, the Lake Paruku project (see Chapter 4), the Canning Stock Route project *Yiwarra Kuju* and the Martu project *We Don't Need a Map*. While each of these projects has art-making and exhibition objectives, they share a deeper cultural purpose focused on the preservation – and active articulation and interpretation – of the Aboriginal master archive in a contemporary context. They also share a collectivist approach that acknowledges the multiple agencies of Indigenous and non-Indigenous knowledge holders, which is not just a feature of Country in the modern world but also a model for the official archive of the Australian nation that resides in its museums and other institutions.

4

SONGLINES
TODAY

I reckon we just gotta move with the times ... Just like the old people,
we are dreaming. We have a new dream with technology. We're using
the newest technology with the oldest culture.

– Curtis Taylor[1]

The dynamics of how the Indigenous archive plays out in Country in contemporary times and in collaboration with Western art and science can only be explained situationally – that is, on Country. The creation of the *Parnkupirti Men's Painting* (2011) reveals the active role of both Indigenous and Western archivists in the interpretation, ongoing maintenance and re-creation of an Indigenous master archive and a third archive. It also reveals how compartmentalised the disciplines are in the Western knowledge system, unlike the integrated Indigenous archive. When the two systems collide, Indigenous cultural practice unsettles the order of Western practice to produce a vehicle for cross-cultural fertilisation so that each can learn from the other.

NEGOTIATED TRUTHS

We can never know what constitutes a so-called 'true' or 'truer' story, a new story or a reclaimed story. Whatever it is, it will take time, with lots of retellings or renegotiations, or both, for a story to gain sufficient authority to fully enter the Aboriginal archive or transcend older interpretations, if indeed it needs to. The negotiations around the creation of the collaborative work *Parnkupirti Men's Painting* give us some powerful insights into the process. This painting hangs in pride of place in the rangers' office in Mulan, a small community in the Kimberley in Western Australia. However, it is not the only 'original': another original hangs in the Nevada Museum of Art in the USA. One painting, two originals. How can this be?

In 2011, deep in the south-east Kimberley by a unique desert lake system called Paruku or Lake Gregory, some thirty people gathered to undertake an artistic collaboration between Indigenous and Western knowledge holders in relation to the complementarity of art and science.

The project was instigated by Western artist Mandy Martin, and the Paruku contingent was coordinated by Western artist and writer Kim Mahood, who was instrumental in a number of ways. William L Fox, director of the Center for Art + Environment at the Nevada Museum of Art, where the work would be displayed, performed the role of Western archivist, recording the cross-cultural transactions as they unfolded in typical Western fashion: with pen and paper. Other members of the party comprised scientists, writers, photographers, Indigenous and non-Indigenous artists, and young Aboriginal rangers from the area. The process behind the making of the work shows the role of the Indigenous archivist and his recasting of the master archive in Country.

Martin was planning a collaborative painting between Indigenous and non-Indigenous artists, and asked Mahood to create a template based on satellite imagery. Mahood had spent some of her childhood growing up at Mongrel Downs (now Tanami Downs) in close contact with the local people, and had worked for many years on cultural and environmental mapping projects with the Walmajarri custodians of Paruku – in particular with elder Veronica Lulu, with whom she now collaborates in an ongoing painting partnership. Mahood would transcribe a satellite map of the environs of Paruku in paint on canvas and work with Lulu and the other custodians to map annual fire activity, lake water levels and any cultural information they chose to put on the canvas. At other times, Mahood and Lulu would sit together in the Kimberley creating the third archive through painting.

After consulting with the custodians about an appropriate site and other relevant matters, Mahood painted a five-panel template of Parnkupirti Creek, the site of an archaeological excavation that was close to the resting place of two ancestral dingoes on their Songline.

Up to this point, most of the participating artists were women. However, once on site and despite the extensive prior consultations, a concurrence of factors caused the senior women to emphatically declare that it was a men's site and that women could not paint the story. The cultural authority of the senior women overrode the authority of Hanson Pye, who was the custodian of that section of the story and had given permission for the collaborative painting at the site. The women handed the panels over to Pye and the rangers to paint. Mahood says the role of the senior Walmajarri women changed from 'artists to custodial sentinels'. The women remained at the consultation site above the dry creek for the first day while the men moved away to do the painting.

None of the rangers were artists except for Pye. However, having been given the directive by the senior women, the men took to the project with enthusiasm. Serendipitously, one of the rangers had a copy of the Paruku Indigenous Protected Area information booklet with him, which had a reproduction of a painting Pye's father had done years earlier about his Dreaming at the site.

Using his father's painting as a template, Pye adapted the iconography of the work to fit the multi-panel format. The open version of the story recounts the final part of the journey of the two dingoes that created the lake, a black male dingo and a white female that have come from the north-east down the two channels of Sturt Creek, meeting at the southern end of the lake and travelling together to Parnkupirti. In this last stage of the journey, they take two ancestral brothers, embodied in Pye's father and uncle, and put them down at locations on Parnkupirti Creek. The nearby twin hills known as Nganpayijarra (two men), which are included in the painting by Pye's father, are also identified with the brothers.

With the essential elements of the painting story laid out, there was a humorous attempt to co-opt Pye's dog into the collaboration by painting his paws and pressing them onto the canvases to create the prints of the two dingoes running side by side along the creek.

This didn't work; the dog refused to cooperate. The rangers then proceeded to paint the prints on individual panels, which resulted in five different renditions of dingo tracks. Dissatisfied with the way this looked, they overpainted the dingo tracks with black paint, obliterating the white creek bed painted by Mahood as part of the original template, painted it white again, and one person painted all the dingo prints. This worked to their satisfaction.

Once the five panels were completed and the dog prints passed muster, the men decided that the painting meant too much to them to part with. They could not send the panels off to Nevada for an exhibition as agreed, as the work had acquired great cultural value through the high degree of community engagement, cross-generational family meaning and revelation involved in its re-creation. Instead, they would do another 'original' to be sent to the exhibition. This decision entailed a further collaboration in which Mahood had the role of creating another set of five canvas panels using the satellite image, and then passing control to the men and withdrawing from sight, like a ritual of another kind. The second painting was completed by Hanson Pye and head ranger Jamie Brown, off-site: the site and the recent experiences were now so firmly in their minds that they did not need to go there again. The mnemonic was in their heads.

While the Walmajarri were engaged in their cultural translation exercise with the Aboriginal archive, William Fox offered his own cultural interpretation. An international expert and writer on art and the environment, and art theory, he observed the overpainting and repainting of the dingo tracks, describing it as 'an act of both aesthetic and metaphoric ownership that made perfect sense'.[2] While acknowledging that the overpainting of part of Mahood's original 'map' template was at odds with his Western view of the authority of the individual artist, he found it 'enthralling to see the men overlay it from edge to edge with their own representation of Country'.[3] Mahood's depiction of the location based on a satellite image reflected a representation of Country through the Western lens of technology and mapping, one with which the Walmajarri rangers were familiar from previous projects. Fox suggests that by overlaying the map with their own painted iconography, the artists were appropriating the Western representation of Country into their own vernacular, drawing together both the ancient story and their contemporary experience of it.[4] Mahood is of the opinion that the decision to overpaint was more likely an aesthetic one, rather than a deliberate erasure of her painted presence, but concedes that she did not witness the process, and that it is open to a number of interpretations.

It is possible that the reason the white was painted out with black paint was not only to remove the dingo prints but, more pertinently, to erase the white woman's participation, or just a woman's participation. Equally, multiple interpretations can coexist, as such articulations by Aboriginal people to non-Aboriginal people in such intense cultural situations are not an exact science. I don't know Pye's views on the matter, but, as Mahood was later called upon to redo the template on the canvases for the 'second original', perhaps the involvement of a woman was not an issue, and the fact that she was a white woman rendered it even less controversial as she was outside the culture. Mahood herself believes that in this context she was simply facilitating the part of the painting that no one else could, and as such was not perceived as a significant element in the process.

This is not the end of the story. As Hanson Pye and the rangers repainted the Parnkupirti story, the two brothers and the two dingoes – four separate entities in the open version of the Dreaming story – morphed into two dingo brothers travelling along Parnkupirti Creek and manifesting as the Nganpayijarra, the two hills that stood close to the location where the dingoes went into the ground. Instead of the white female dingo and the black male dingo, the white dingo became the older brother and the black dingo became the younger brother, Hanson Pye's father.

Further negotiations took place when Pye, a natural storyteller, was speaking about the Paruku project in front of an eager group of listeners at the Araluen Arts Centre in Alice Springs. He told his version of the story, as it had revealed itself to him on the day at Parnkupirti: using his father's painting as a template, the young men at hand to paint the story, the interested and sympathetic *kartiya* (white people) participating in the process, all of it authorised and kept safe by the senior women. In attendance was Evelyn Clancy, an old aunty with significant cultural authority who had been one of the 'custodial sentinels' at the creek bed. She felt that Pye's transformation was a step too far, and without regard to the audience, or Pye's potential embarrassment, she pulled him up on the spot, saying, 'No! No! Not the right story!' Mahood's reading was that Pye was 'transfixed by the symmetry of the two hills, the two brothers, the two dingoes and the site, and aided by his father's painting in the booklet, in his mind this version had usurped the other'.[5] Though Pye retreated from his telling of this version at the arts centre in response to the aunty's interjection, and no doubt out of respect for her cultural authority, Mahood reckons that this newer story is now so lodged in him after such a transformative experience that this rendition may potentially supplant the other.

We will never know the true story – and we don't need to know. With sufficient tellings it will re-enter the archive via the paintings that now exist as documented evidence, and the many more paintings and stories they will probably spawn. This story at Paruku reveals and reinforces a number of points about the apparent mutability and immutability of the Aboriginal archive. Pye renewed and re-created the archive in the process of accessing it. The painting as an archival document will be read back into the Country in its retelling in one or more ways.

We may well ask how this accords with the view that the Dreaming is immutable and cannot be changed by humans. The short answer is that the Dreaming functions at many levels. At its deepest level, it is not ambiguous or mutable. This deep meaning sets the boundaries within which there is some mobility of interpretation at the narrative or storytelling level. The story shifts in the hands of different storytellers, in different circumstances, at different times, with different groupings of people, at different sites, but the 'inside' essence, or the metadata, is unchangeable. This shifting and movement arising from a variety of cultural engagements keeps the Dreaming alive and keeps the archive active, relevant and memorable.

SONGLINES GREAT AND SMALL

Some stories referred to as Songlines, the Dreaming or Dreaming tracks are contained and confined to a small area or site and do not travel far over Country. You may be familiar with expressions like Wallaby Dreaming or Yam Dreaming. These are more likely to be localised Dreamings that assist in hunting and harvesting in an area. The ceremonies and songs are ways of acknowledging the wallaby and yam ancestors, which aids in the increase of supply. However, Songlines like the Seven Sisters are epic. They stretch across the entire continent like a web of interconnecting pathways encompassing multiple sites, unlike the two dingoes story with its focus on that creek, that lake and those two hills. The Seven Sisters saga, associated with Orion and the Pleiades, where the cosmological drama of the story continues from the terrestrial one, is told around the world, wherever the constellation and star cluster are visible.

At Kuru Ala, some 200 kilometres from Papulankutja (Blackstone) or twelve hours' drive west of Alice Springs in the Great Victoria Desert, lies an area comprising a collection of sites rich with the imprint of the Kungkarrangkalpa, or the Seven Sisters. Their presence, and that of their relentless pursuer Wati Nyiru, who harmed the eldest sister, is so palpable at Kuru Ala that Anangu speak in hushed tones there for fear of disturbing him and for other reasons not disclosed.

As part of the Songlines project, we camped at Kuru Ala in April 2014 and again in August 2015. Some thirty traditional Seven Sisters custodians from the Ngaanyatjarra, Pitjantjatjara and Yankunytjatjara (NPY) language groups got their long-awaited trip back to Country, where they gathered to bring 'the stories up from Country', to regenerate the archive and engage in knowledge transfer. Unlike what had happened with previous generations, this knowledge transfer was not with the younger generation on Country but with anthropologists, academics and museum curators. The custodians had engaged Western knowledge holders to document the knowledge by exploiting the very technologies that were distracting their youth from being with them on this and other trips over the past decade.

Over many days at Kuru Ala, which means 'eyes open', the custodians walked the sites telling stories, singing songs and touching places as they reconnected. An authorised few painted their breasts with circles of white ochre, replicating natural markings on the rocks believed to be from smoke used by the younger sisters to heal the eldest sister, who was harmed by Wati Nyiru at this place.[6] The knowledge-laden features of the land that formed the backdrop provided the cue for the performers of the dance. Like a time-lapse re-enactment staged in Country, the seven elders – painted up and wearing headpieces and black skirts – filed through the grass, forever vigilant of Wati Nyiru, who darted from rock to tree, hiding as he went or sitting atop a rock to survey the land for sight of them. Likewise, the elders stopped and huddled with their backs to each other and hands shielding their eyes as they peered into the distance, scanning for their relentless pursuer. Eventually the sisters descended into a gully and disappeared from sight. Rising some 20 to 30 metres from the gully floor was the face of their pursuer, deeply gouged into the craggy rock with pronounced eye sockets squinting cat-like.

There was no escape. Wati Nyiru transformed into a python, leaving a clearly defined crevice in the rock face – evidence of where he slithered down before slipping into the waterhole at the base of the escarpment, where the sisters had come to hunt and gather. They were, as he intended, attracted by the promise of snake meat, which was good tucker. But the eldest sister was alert to the tricky ways of Wati Nyiru the shapeshifter, who was continually transforming into desirable foods to lure the sisters to him. Instead of catching the snake to cook and consume, as he hoped, the sisters caught him and threw him into the sky, from where he travelled to another site called Kulyuru, some 100 kilometres to the west. Here, the encounters between the sisters and Wati Nyiru in his snake guise continued.

Wati Nyiru's face in the rock formation at Kuru Ala

The tableau of dance across Country was captured on film for the Seven Sisters project and exhibition, as it had been a number of times before. Later, on canvas, the story was painted into being, simultaneously strengthening it for reabsorption into the site and spiritually caring for Country. The painting as ceremony was ritually supervised by bosses and managers (known as *Kurdu* and *Kuralangu* in other parts of the desert). The artist-archivists engaging in the painting ceremony had particular relationships to each other, to the story and to the site, which governed the orchestration of what followed. With so many painters involved – six female and one male – and with the complexity of kinship and familial relationships, I expected extensive and time-consuming negotiations to occur, to determine who would sit where and who would paint what. Instead, everyone quietly and purposefully formed themselves around the canvas according to their relationships, and spatially oriented themselves to the particular sites they were recording and connected to.

Mrs Woods, who has since passed away but was then believed to be in her nineties, was the most senior custodian on the day. She was strong in this story, taking the lead role for the women's side. Her knowledge of the dance and the Country was profound and apparently unrivalled. Anthropologist Bryony Nicholson described how in the past Mrs Woods had danced the most potent parts of this Tjukurrpa along with the late Mrs Miller, with drama and undisputed authority. Facing the back of Mrs Woods was the monumental rock formation with the face of Wati Nyiru. Mrs Woods depicted him on the canvas with large circles, like eyes, suggesting not only his watchfulness but also the acts that she used to so dramatically perform. Robert Woods, Mrs Woods' son by kinship, positioned himself on the adjacent corner of the canvas, where he was boss of the men's part of the story. He faced the site of the carpet snake that was one of Wati Nyiru's many guises (with apparent reference to his intent to wrongfully make the sisters his wives). Between them, and flanking Mrs Woods, were her daughters, half-sisters Anawari Mitchell and Angilyiya Mitchell, with the former telling the story of catching the 'carpet snake' for the sisters to consume and enable Wati Nyiru to possess them. The latter painted the story of strengthening and healing the damaged and dying sister by feeding her meat (*kuka*) and dancing up healing power, as described previously. Beside Robert Woods was Jennifer Mitchell, Mrs Woods' other daughter and Robert's half-sister, who painted the place of healing. Sitting separately on the remaining side of the canvas were Lalla West and Lesley Laidlaw, representatives from a different but related family; they claim connection to the site because their mother, Nyumitja Laidlaw, was born near Kuru Ala, constituting one of the strongest claims to place. The Woods–Mitchell family were not born there, but their rights were hereditary and their knowledge strong as a consequence of ongoing engagement with the place, keeping the story alive.

For the painting to have cultural authority as a document of value, both sets of knowledge holders needed to be part of the telling. The selection of artists to paint that story at that time in that place was subject to a shifting hierarchy, encompassing cultural, spatial, temporal and genealogical factors that are always present and inform every work to some degree. For example, at this same site in 2011, an apparent disagreement between knowledge, experience and antecedence from family members born at Kuru Ala came to a head. There was an impasse between people who knew the story versus a particular member of Nyumitja's family, when consensus was needed on who should or could dance the story. It was finally resolved through what Nicholson, who was present, described as 'ceremonial conflict resolution that resulted in a targeted, intensive knowledge transfer session for this person who now has the confidence to dance this story and is acknowledged by all the women as being able to do so'.[7]

The inclusion of Lesley Laidlaw as a painter on this canvas in 2015 was an outcome of these negotiations four years earlier, when her mother Nyumitja's rights were reconfirmed. Laidlaw appears not to have really taken on this Tjukurrpa or the dancing for this place. Instead, she seemed more comfortable acknowledging her mother's connection than asserting her own. Based on precedence and inherited rights, her family had to have a seat at the table to do the story the proper way.

This example not only hints at the complexity of accessing, affirming and transmitting archival knowledge in multiple ways but, more precisely, how the bona fides of the archivist for the Aboriginal archive are established through family lineage. In Western archival terms, it could loosely be seen as a form of validation of the documentation through cross-referencing.

Artists can also access the Aboriginal archive remotely, a facility that was active for centuries prior to the new technologies of today – a kind of wi-fi of the cosmological variety, putting a new twist on cloud platforms. On another desert research trip with Anangu on the APY Lands far to the west of Kuru Ala, at the top of South Australia near the tri-state border, the cue for the Seven Sisters saga was the Orion constellation and Pleiades star cluster canopied above, rather than the surrounding landscape.

In September 2012, in an isolated sandy riverbed in a remote region beyond Ernabella (Pukatja), some fifty Anangu people gathered to do *inma* (performance) for an episode of the Seven Sisters story. Week-long rehearsals were underway in preparation for a public performance at the National Museum of Australia as part of Canberra's centennial year of celebrations, interrupted only by that other great celebration on the lands at that time of year: an Australian Rules football grand final. After sundown, when full dress rehearsals took place, the inky nights were punctuated by tongues of flame from the crackling fires and the glistening bodies of the dancers. The rhythm of walking Country as a way of remembering was emulated in the rhythm of dance movements as the dancers took the song into their bodies, informing the dance and the vocalisations, unifying past, present and place with the human and the ancestral. The collective bank of stories was sung out, day after day, night after night, recalling deeply embedded places in the mind, until by the last night the performance took on an edge not seen before. A senior traditional owner of the episode being performed was quivering and shuddering on the ground as if in her death throes after being harmed by Wati Nyiru. The younger sisters were protectively circling in movements and gestures of mourning and healing. Endless negotiations on the deepening story occurred as different parts and snippets of knowledge were jigsawed back into place.

In performances, edible plants and animals are often named from half-remembered songs as the Songline travelled from water source to water source. Literally and metaphorically, the learning of ecology, geology, botany, medicine and husbandry is revealed, along with codes of behaviour and roles and responsibilities in performances such as these. This is how Anangu know their Country. This is what they learn from the archive and what they read back into the archive through a process of curating, painting, song and dance.

Mirrored in the night sky, with a degree of clarity only experienced in the desert, the saga of Wati Nyiru and the Seven Sisters continues – then as now, 'as above, so below'. Each night, as Orion and the Pleiades come into view, the archive is revived. They are a constant reminder of the knowledge contained in this narrative, replicated in the Pleiades star cluster seen as the Seven Sisters, and the Orion constellation as Wati Nyiru.

5

SONGLINES AND SYNAPSES

*This kujika is for us, the Mambaliya kujika is ours. We follow it from
Nungkajabarra, there in the east and then we come from the east
through Mukarrala, and then down to the river at Milibundurra, and
then we follow it by way of the river bank to Rrungun – it is a creek –
we travel up the creek and we come to Nyamurri. We are naming
the Spotted Nightjar and the Crow at that place. All right, onward
we go: we are following that kujika eastwards; we are following
the kujika south-east and pass through Warrakundanarra, then
Anthawaliyangka and then Arrakarrala; we are ascending eastwards,
this way eastwards through the messmate tree country, all the way east
to Nganjarrnganjarra, then there is Rungkurr and Kujulu, and then
the kujika is rising up to Jarramba and travels east to Alakalangaya.
It is here we are naming that Rainbow Serpent, the one that comes
from the east – we are naming him the Stranger. Then we are going
southwards, following southwards all the way to Yarrambala – that
is the name of the place – Yarrambala. Onwards and southwards,
and there we are going around and around on the south-west side of*

Wumayalinja. It is there that our senior paternal grandfather, that snake, that Blind Rainbow Serpent, was standing.

[Dinny] narrated not from the perspective of a mere observer but as if located within the kujika itself and moving with it, over the savannah country, into the creeks and lagoons, listening to and observing the conversations between Ancestral beings that resonated still in the country. It was as if the kujika carried his consciousness of the country in its own.

– John Bradley, quoting Dinny McDinny[1]

Songlines are an embodied knowledge system: knowledge is carried by the human body and transmitted to others, primarily through performance prompted by actual and visualised features of the country.

Those of us who have spent our lives immersed in writing may feel Songlines are an alien system – one for them, not us, but we would be wrong to think that way. We can only glimpse the intellectual and emotional investment of an Aboriginal person who has spent their whole life learning in Country, but even that glimpse can offer us a precious lesson.

Indigenous cultures are often referred to as 'non-literate' because they don't have a form of writing that can be instantly recognised by

Western observers. But using the term 'non-literate' disguises the fact that Indigenous cultures have an alternative to conventional literacy known as orality, a way of archiving knowledge in the landscape, activated through performance. It is therefore preferable to refer to such cultures as 'oral'. Songlines are the chief vehicle of orality.

All humans, whatever their culture, are inhibited by an unreliable memory. Indigenous cultures are dependent on their memories for everything they know. They use a whole suite of alternatives to literacy to ensure that the encyclopedia of knowledge they have built up over tens of thousands of years is maintained and constantly updated. Without this knowledge, the people simply would not have survived, physically or culturally.

If we used standard Western encyclopedic terms for the knowledge that can be retrieved from the Songlines, the headings would include animals, plants, genealogies, geology, climate and seasons, land management, geography, astronomy, calendars, natural resources, ecology, religion, laws and ethics, among many others. Exploring just one topic – say, animals – will reveal hundreds of species. Indigenous people recognise not only the animals that Western science classifies as mammals, like the kangaroos, but also all the birds, fish, reptiles, amphibians and the hundreds upon hundreds of invertebrates.

The Indigenous encyclopedia has been memorised over thousands of generations, and constantly refined. Scientists have verified repeatedly that some of the stories date back tens of thousands of years. Without robust memory methods, it would be impossible to store such a vast array of knowledge in memory.

Each generation can't rediscover the information. Testing every plant in the environment to find which can be used for food, medicine, shelter, tools and an abundance of materials is impossible. That amazing feat is all down to Songlines. But how does a Songline actually work? And how can non-Indigenous cultures learn from the world's oldest living culture to use the third archive? The answer lies in looking at the human brain and how it stores memory.

SONGLINES ARE FOR EVERYONE

All knowledge, no matter where you store it, is based on memory. It is as if Aboriginal cultures read modern neuroscience and created a knowledge system to match. In truth, the system evolved over thousands of years, constantly being tested and perfected with use. Songlines optimise the way human memory works.

Cells are usually thought of as microscopic entities, but some cells in the human body can be nearly a metre long, although only a few microns wide. They are neurons: specialised cells that make up the nervous system and transmit information around our bodies. Neurons combine in their billions to form the nervous system.

The main area of the brain for learning and for converting short-term to long-term memory is the hippocampus. You physically change your brain with everything you learn. This ability of the brain to change is known as plasticity. It used to be thought that the brain was hardwired from a young age, but recent research has shown that plasticity lasts throughout life. It is a matter of exercising your brain the same way you exercise all your other muscles.

Every time you learn something, new physical neural pathways are established in your brain – the memory is actually physically laid down. If you don't reinforce it fairly quickly, then you will lose access to that memory even if it is still hanging around somewhere. If you reinforce it and make sure you have a way of calling it back, it will be yours forever.

This is where all the features of Songlines come into play. The brain is particularly good at associating memories with music, dance and art, and it is spectacularly good at associating memory with places. And it needs novelty: your brain simply doesn't remember things that are abstract or dull. Exploring the cognitive elements that are active when Indigenous people engage with their Songlines is very revealing. Each element of the performance of the Songlines can be linked to specific valuable neurological processes. In combination, these elements form a powerful knowledge system applicable to any human brain.

The vital element is the way in which Songlines call up Country. A Songline presents a structure for knowledge that is literally grounded in the landscape. As described by Yanyuwa man Dinny McDinny at the beginning of this chapter, when an Aboriginal person is engaged with a Songline, they are mentally in the physical space where the actions of the ancestors occurred. It becomes even more extraordinary when you consider that there are over 800 kilometres of Songlines known by the Yanyuwa people alone.

Very recent research on the relationship between space and memory earned scientists Edvard Moser, May-Britt Moser and John O'Keefe the 2014 Nobel Prize in Physiology or Medicine. They showed that entorhinal grid cells constitute a positioning system in the brain and encode a cognitive representation of the physical space you inhabit – and they are doing it all the time.

Memories are stored in the brain in a kind of spatial map. The hippocampus gets particularly active when learning spatial knowledge, so any knowledge encoded by using physical locations will be remembered far more easily than information that has no physical grounding. Memories that piggyback on the hippocampus's ability to remember space can become very strong: any events we associate with specific locations at a given time can gain this potency.

Familiar environments are recorded in our brains as actual physical pathways made of neurons. Anyone who knows their home, school, workplace or neighbourhood already has a landscape that they can use to start taking advantage of this natural ability. The more you engage with your personal landscape, the more familiar it becomes and the more robustly it is represented in the physical structures of your brain.

Neurons in the hippocampus will associate abstract knowledge, not just experiences, with any place where that knowledge is talked about at the same time as the place is evoked. This is what neuroscientists call a 'temporal snapshot'. So being at a particular location, or imagining yourself there, at the same time as you learn something new enables extremely robust memory by associating events with the familiar locations in the landscape. Concentrate on imagining Isaac Newton standing at your front gate, and your brain will associate him permanently with that location. We explore exactly how to use this ability in your own life in Chapter 10.

Indigenous people's use of the landscape is enhanced by the fact that a sequenced story emerges as you move through the spaces, and the story is further enhanced by the use of song and movements, including dance. This vivid knowledge space is then reproduced in art and repeated through ceremony. As every performance is slightly different, the brain is constantly exposed to novelty. There is emotional investment in the performance, but also times when singing the names evokes imagination to revisit the story.

Upon this firm foundation, senior members of the community provide commentary, not only to teach but also to use restricted knowledge to maintain accuracy. By keeping knowledge secret from those not yet ready to receive and protect it, they can ensure that every repetition of the story is accurate. That can't be done in a free-for-all chat. This foundation is used as a base on which to layer ever more complex knowledge of the Songline.

The fact that Aboriginal people know their Country intimately has granted them an invaluable tool for long-term memory to learn new knowledge. It is no surprise that Indigenous cultures all over the world independently created knowledge systems based on events associated with their physical landscape, something we examine further in Chapter 7.

When a long time has elapsed since you last studied particular information, it is likely you will forget what you have learnt. The research also shows that if your brain is given some kind of cue, it will often recall information you think you have forgotten. Old memories can be retrieved. By associating knowledge with locations in Country, Aboriginal people have those cues permanently in place.

The more distinctive a cue, the more likely it is to work. The way in which Songlines are mapped onto a sequence of distinctive locations, each separated from the other, is the optimum set of cues.

SINGING UP COUNTRY: TAKING IT INSIDE

Our brains love narrative. We are a storytelling species. By linking landscape locations through story, Songlines call on this intrinsic trait to increase the likelihood that no location is lost and that the associated knowledge is retained. Each episode in the Songline is vivid and distinct, increasing the unique identification of the place in Country, which means that the chance of confusing one location with another is further reduced.

Central to performances are songs. As senior Yanyuwa woman Eileen McDinny explains, 'Everything got a song, no matter how little, it's in the song – name of plant, birds, animal, country, people, everything got a song.'[2]

The research on the impact of music on memory is substantial and shows that music is a powerful mnemonic device primarily because songs are more memorable than text. If the music is already familiar, then it also invokes a strong sense of knowing, of understanding. The research on music and memory also shows clearly that music causes an emotional response, and being emotionally engaged makes any information much more memorable. Music awakens us, arouses us, keeps our attention. Music is far more engaging than spoken or written text, so song is an invaluable tool with which to archive information.

The songs associated with the Songlines tell the stories, such as that of the Seven Sisters and their pursuer. But songs also encode other meanings, storing vast amounts of knowledge about the environment, culture and law. And the emotional songs that form an integral part of the Songlines are performed, not simply sung. For example, detailed research has been done on the Yankunytjatjara songs containing extensive knowledge of over 100 of the plants the Yankunytjatjara people use. The translator noted that the information couldn't be fully recorded in writing because then 'the stories lack the performance quality that was so much a part of the way they were told'.[3]

Research that analysed 174 of the much larger body of songs of the Australian Dyirbal song specialists showed that the songs encode their complex kinship system, social responsibilities, birds, mammals, fish, insects, reptiles, techniques for hunting and fishing, places and the land, the cause of thunder, the causes and cures of illness, love, grief and bravery, plus historical events of both the distant past and quite recent times.[4]

Even technical processes are reliably recorded in songs that are sung while work is being done. The Haya of north-western Tanzania chant sexually explicit rhythms and movements to dictate every phase of ironworking. The knowledge has been made particularly memorable by using the human reproductive cycle as a metaphor for the ironworking phases.[5]

Indigenous cultures all over the world record their family relationships in song in ways that are much more extensive than simple written family trees. These genealogies are so complex that they are very difficult for anthropologists from Western cultures to understand. In West Africa, there are people who specialise in reciting genealogies. The long narrative of history and genealogy sung by Griot (male) and sometimes by Griotte (female) can take hours, even days, to sing and requires years of intensive study to master.[6]

Enacting knowledge hugely increases recall, especially when the movement is in the form of dance accompanying song. It is a whole-body transmission where the message is conveyed through sound, rhythm, tone, body action, beat and words. A stationary audience watching a few performers will learn far less than Aboriginal people do when they see Aboriginal performances that involve everyone present to some degree. The knowledge is much more widely experienced by Aboriginal people, at a deep and memorable level.

Dance also involves exercise. Neurogenesis is the creation of new neurons, which enhances the brain's plasticity. Exercise enhances neurogenesis, so performing knowledge is the optimum way to engage the brain in storing new information for the long term.

There is another advantage in using dance: some things are much better represented by movement than writing. For example, dances can depict animal behaviour and tactics for the hunt in a way no words can.

Neurons in the brain are connected via minute gaps between the synapses. Neurons communicate chemically across the synapses, creating the neural networks that store memory. Your brain will constantly strengthen the synapses that are most active. Dynamic performance of emotionally engaging stories is exactly what your brain needs to be at its most receptive. Aboriginal performance of Songlines could not have evolved into a more effective knowledge system.

It is important that the knowledge is performed repeatedly. There needs to be a ceremonial cycle or some other process to ensure that the knowledge is revisited regularly, ensuring songs are encoded deep within the brain's networks. But repetition is only helpful when you are thinking about meaning. The way each performance is different and vibrant, but the content remains constant, is exactly what neuroscience suggests is the optimum. Novelty is a great trigger for neurogenesis. The brain loves something that is different, while it ignores the very familiar. Every Aboriginal performer brings a new interpretation to the songs without corrupting the original message. This ensures repetition without boredom. Because performances on Country cause every individual to be engaged with what is happening, learning for the young is optimised and recall by the older performers is reinforced.

To maximise neurogenesis, you want to be thinking new and creative ideas and exciting your brain. If the ancestors created the Songlines about ordinary people engaged in ordinary daily life, then they wouldn't have created the vivid knowledge system that exists. For example, in the Seven Sisters Songline, exceptional women are being chased by a relentless pursuer through a wildly variable landscape, with the stories told by song and enacted through performance.

As if the performance of the knowledge system encoding the Songlines isn't enough, further devices are used to ensure that the encyclopedia that is the landscape is even more strongly archived. Art is an extraordinarily powerful mnemonic device, so valuable that we've devoted all of Chapter 9 to this topic.

The brain wants novelty, but the neuroscience also says that associating something with knowledge that is already familiar, such as the landscape, will grant hooks and cues to memories that may appear forgotten. Songlines offer exactly this seemingly incompatible combination of circumstances.

THE POWER OF LAYERED KNOWLEDGE

It is important that what you learn when you are young is retained throughout your life with ever-increasing complexity added. Recent research has shown that elusive brain plasticity, once thought to be the great gift of the young, is on offer throughout life – even into old age. But to retain knowledge and build upon it you must constantly revisit it. Aboriginal people perform ceremonies repeatedly throughout their life, both on Country and in their mind.

As we show in Chapter 6, many stories have been maintained accurately over tens of thousands of years, and much of the knowledge is restricted to certain groups within the social structure. Some is women's business, some is men's. Some knowledge is conveyed to the young, while other insights require initiation at various levels before being revealed. The social structures ensure accuracy of the knowledge, which could never be achieved by simply relying on unreliable human memories. Information is easily corrupted when it is repeated from one person to another, even in a matter of minutes. By restricting knowledge to those who are ready for it, and then ensuring that it is repeated accurately, seemingly impossible feats of accurate retention can be achieved.

Often a senior member of a community may add narrative or correct details during a performance. This process ensures accuracy but also reinforces the details in the minds of those performing it. Aboriginal people spend much time discussing the stories encoded in their Songlines. These discussions, often referred to as commentaries, add novelty and depth to the memory in the people's cognitive archives. It is upon the immutable structure of Country that layer upon layer of interwoven knowledge, commentary, philosophy, debate and higher levels of learning can be constructed.

In order to recall all the knowledge encoded in the Songlines, the performers do not need to be at the actual location in Country: Country is so much a part of who they are that they can call on it anytime and draw from it the knowledge they need. In fact, they don't ever need to have been to the Country because the songs can draw the images so vividly. For example, many of the sites celebrated in the ceremonies of the Antikirinja women of Central Australia tell of places that were neither in traditional Antikirinja Country nor in the Country in which the performers currently reside, yet they have extensive knowledge of the sites and the routes covered by the ancestral journeys.[7]

ANCIENT GREEK ORATORS AND MEMORY CHAMPIONS

Credit for a memory system built on the landscape is almost always given to the ancient Greeks. However, the system most likely evolved from the oral tradition of their forebears long before writing – an oral tradition that has now been overwritten. The famed 'memory palaces' of the ancient Greeks are simplified versions of Songlines. The methods are so robust that all contemporary memory champions embed their memory feats in landscape palaces. But they are silent palaces, without song and without ceremony.

From around 800 BCE, the time of Homer, ancient Greek and Roman cultures flourished. There were no books, so the memories of the great orators served as encyclopedias for the entire population. It is recorded that Homer could recite all 16,000 verses of *The Iliad* from memory, which would have taken him at least four long evenings of non-stop performance. Other bards of his time would imitate him telling his great stories. Cicero and Quintilian, around the time of Christ, and, later, Augustine of Hippo were the pop stars of their day, with audiences clamouring to hear dramatic renditions of their lengthy speeches.

The orators would break up their speeches into short sections and walk around a familiar physical space, such as a building or streetscape, and as they did so they would allocate each part of the speech to a distinctive location on their route. We know about these memory techniques because of a famous textbook used for hundreds of years, the *Rhetorica ad Herennium*, written by an anonymous author and dedicated to a now-forgotten man called Herennius.

The *Rhetorica ad Herennium* teaches that each location should be distinctive and that the locations should be in a definite sequence. The route should be away from where the orator lives because otherwise he will be easily distracted from his purpose. Each location should be a moderate size and a moderate distance from the other locations. When giving his performance, the orator should imagine himself walking around the building or down the street, recalling each of the verses in order as he went. The knowledge he associates with each location should be as striking and dramatic, as vibrant and active and as full of characters as possible. There should be heroes and trauma, disasters and great feats, all of which make the story easier to remember.

The *Rhetorica ad Herennium* was teaching the orators to create what we in Australia call Songlines. This technique is known as the method of loci – that is, the method of using locations for memory. It was so successful that it was taught in all schools for thousands of years, right into medieval and Renaissance times. Over the centuries, more and more elaborate buildings, churches and theatres were used, sometimes existing only in the imagination of the user. The memory spaces, real and imagined, became known as memory palaces and are still used by a select few today.

For example, participants in contemporary memory championships might be required to very rapidly memorise the order of a shuffled deck of cards, hundreds of words, long lists of numbers and other abstract information. The competitors almost all employ the method of loci, walking their homes or churches, grand buildings or public spaces in their imagination. To memorise the order of a shuffled deck of playing cards, a competitor assigns each card a character. They then associate a sequence of stories about these characters in the locations of a memory palace they have created for the purpose. They do the same with numbers, giving each group of numbers a character and again using stories and memory palaces.

Eight-time world memory champion Dominic O'Brien developed his own version, not realising it had been used throughout history. He referred to it as 'the journey method', a much more accurate description of what it feels like to walk spaces in your imagination.[8]

DO THEY HAVE BETTER BRAINS?

Are the brains of Aboriginal elders, ancient Greek orators and memory champions special in some way?

There is no research on the brains of Indigenous elders or ancient Greeks, but there are a number of studies of the brains of world memory champions. The results show that their superior memory is not because they were born more intelligent nor that their brain has special structural differences. Their abilities are almost exclusively because they have trained their memory using the techniques taught so long ago in that Greek textbook. All research to date offers compelling evidence that dramatic improvements in memory are possible for anyone who is willing to learn and practise these memory techniques. It is training that alters the brain's neural networks, and training that so dramatically increases memory performance.

To date, most people in Western society have not used all the memory options available to them. They have not taken advantage of the techniques demonstrated so beautifully in the Songlines. Our memories are an under-utilised resource in which ancient knowledge systems have been supplanted by Western knowledge systems, which outsource much of our knowledge to books and technology. We can have both. We can have the Indigenous archive so skilfully optimised over millennia and demonstrated in the Songlines, and we can use the Western archive so wonderfully recorded in writing and technology. We can have a third archive, combining the best from both.

6

SONGLINES SPIRAL FOREVER

Songspirals are often called Songlines or song cycles. ... we call them songspirals as they spiral out and spiral in, they go up and down, round and round, forever. They are a line within a circle. They are infinite. They spiral, connecting and remaking. They twist and turn, they move and loop. This is like all our songs. Our songs are not a straight line. They do not move in one direction through time and space. They are a map we follow through Country as they connect to other clans. Everything is connected, layered with beauty. Each time we sing our song spirals we learn more, go deeper, spiral in and spiral out ...

Songspirals have been here a long time. Forever. They are Yolŋu Law. They bring us into being and they link us to the land, to Country. They come from the land and they create it too. It's not just that song spirals created our land a long time ago, but they keep on creating it, and us, and everything in our Country.

– Gay'wu Group of Women[1]

It is easier for those of us used to linear writing and paper maps to think of Songlines as paths through the forest, such that we would walk along on a day in the bush. For Aboriginal people, these tracks are far more complex. They weave across the entire nation and exist in a more multidimensional way than a line that can be measured in kilometres. It is impossible to travel all the Songlines as the area they cover is too vast. Some are still known; others have been lost.

SPACE IS EVERYWHERE AND TIME IS 'EVERYWHEN'

The massive Australian continent is overwritten by a mesh of complex Songlines covering nearly 8 million square kilometres. Each section is maintained and controlled by the local traditional owners but also shared when appropriate. Australian Songlines are without doubt the largest memory palace ever used.

When trying to conceive of the size of just one Songline, such as that of the Seven Sisters, we must consider that it also includes the sky above Country. It is then truly 'everywhere' and unable to be quantified in the Western way of thinking.

But it is more than that. When we walk through an area of bush, we are walking in the present and most of our thoughts are in the present, even though we may consider the past and the future as we stroll along. Many Aboriginal people when they walk on Country, however, experience the past of the ancestors and every time span that has existed and will ever exist. Anthropologist WEH Stanner coined the expression 'everywhen' when he was grappling with this Aboriginal sense of time and place.[2]

The Anangu group describe their Tjukurpa as referring to the past and the future at the same time as the enduring present. Their stories talk about the beginning of time, when ancestral beings first created the world and all the teachings inscribed by them, but also about everything that has happened since. The Anangu also explain how Tjukurpa stories are used like maps, describing how to travel from one place to another but also, critically, where and when to find water and food. Knowledge contained in the stories deepens and enlarges over time for those who continue to engage with law and culture on Country. Different ways of learning are evolving, including access to knowledge in digital forms through Aboriginal-managed archives such as Ara Irititja. The Songlines are never-ending but firm foundations for lifelong learning.

SONGLINES ARE ROBUST YET DYNAMIC

That Songlines emerged from the depths of time doesn't mean that Aboriginal culture is static. Time is not divided into past, present and future. A saying oft-repeated by Aboriginal people describes time cycles and spirals: when you look behind you, you see the future in your footprints. Every performance brings out each person's different level of understanding and learning. Performances tell a story in motion that is basically immutable, but the way a performer colours that story changes with the storyteller.

You can imagine this much like the body of a singer moving with a song. Every human who ever enacted a particular Songline had the same set of bones, but the way their flesh was distributed on those bones and their skin tone and the colour of their hair and costume varied. So it is with Songlines. The ancestors laid down the initial tracks, the songs and dances and knowledge, but each player intensifies the Songlines through their own level of understanding and interpretation. The Songlines are dynamic, and as robust as the country itself.

Part of the Songlines that is easy to imagine is the Anangu Tjukurpa that travels around the base of the huge monolith Uluru. As you walk the more than 10 kilometres around the base of the rock, its bulk, crevices and markings reveal location after location where the knowledge of the Kuniya-Liru Tjukurpa (female python and poison snake men) and the Mala Tjukurpa (rufous hare-wallaby and Walmalla war party from the south-west) is stored through the stories that have been passed down throughout time. Because this Tjukurpa remains relevant today, tourists have been banned from freely walking around and on Uluru. That is only a small portion of the Tjukurpa for this area. Like in a relay, the baton is passed on, extending everywhere and existing in the everywhen.

It is this longevity of relationship with Country that enabled Aboriginal people to make land claims. For example, in 2000 the Yanyuwa people made a claim on Kangaroo Island in the Northern Territory. The Yanyuwa from Borroloola sang their *Kujika*, their Songlines, and performed it publicly in the land-claim court. This demonstrated not only their knowledge and connection to Country but, critically, their continuing link to the ancient past and the ancestors. It is through the Kujika that the local traditional owners could lay claim to the land in Western terms. In Australian

Aboriginal terms, they do not own the land; the land owns them. They are the custodians with the responsibility to care for Country.

Just how old is the relationship? From a Western perspective, Aboriginal occupation of Australia is known to date from at least 65,000 years ago. To put that in a global context, ancient Greece existed only a few thousand years ago and the pyramids and Stonehenge are a mere 5000 years old. Although still much debated by archaeologists, it is currently thought that the first humans to reach the Americas arrived about 15,000 years ago. There is no contemporary African culture that can be traced back as far as those in Australia.

A culture requires more than a genetic link: it requires evidence of ceremony, occupation and knowledge passed down for all that time. It is only in the past few decades that Western science has started to catch up on what Aboriginal people have so often told us. There is unequivocal scientific evidence confirming a continuous culture dating back at least 15,000 years. It is likely that further scientific work will push that date back further, closer to the 65,000 years Aboriginal cultures have been present in Australia.

How have anthropologists understood what Aboriginal people have been saying about their culture dating back so long?

So far, the earliest Australian rock engravings to be dated were created around 30,000 years ago. There is older rock art in Europe, but none of the cultures who painted it have survived to explain it to us. Unfortunately, rock engravings erode and the pigments in paintings wear away. However, the earliest Australian rock art shows geometric forms, including pecked circles, lines and animal footprints that continue in the same form, repeated in a huge range of contexts, right up to the present day.[3]

That the same motifs appear from so very long ago does not mean that their meanings have not changed and adapted to the contemporary needs of the artists. As we discuss further in Chapter 9, using abstract designs enables a greater complexity to be encoded than do representational images alone. Simpler images are also easier to replicate so the meanings can be spread throughout the local community and transferred into the broader culture. What is important is that the motifs have appeared consistently and continuously for at least 30,000 years. This indicates a continuing tradition, exactly as described when Indigenous people talk of their Songlines.

KNOWLEDGE MUST BE STORED FOR CONSTANT USE

It would not be possible to discover the vast store of knowledge of every animal and plant, every weather condition and every location, all the rules and regulations and genealogies and the way to manage the land, if you had to rediscover it every time the knowledge was needed. There is much too much to learn even in a few generations. It has to be stored in the oral tradition.

Only with complete and accurate knowledge of the ecosystem and seasons could Indigenous people be sure of a well-fed and sustainable life. Consider the cycad *Macrozamia moorei*. Eating fresh cycad seeds will kill you very quickly. Yet cycads are a very high-yielding source of carbohydrate and protein, and the ceremonial gatherings of some Aboriginal cultures are totally dependent on cycad seeds for feeding the large group who meet for weeks or months at a time. To make the seeds safe takes days of preparation.

It is obvious that these cultures must have been taught this information by previous generations. Somewhere, somehow, at some time, testing showed that the seeds were deadly and to be avoided at all costs. But then someone discovered that leaching them in water for four days made them not only safe but hugely sustaining when ground into flour and made into bread. Alternatively, the kernels could be fermented over a number of months in large containers or pits, and the results were delicious.

By regularly burning stands of cycads, the land could be managed in such a way that competing vegetation was eliminated and kernel production massively increased. The Aboriginal knowledge included how to ensure a whole stand of cycads would ripen at the same time, ready to feed the huge numbers attending the ceremonial gatherings. This knowledge was embedded in the Songlines and linked to a specific site. The stories would tell of how an ancestor got sick and what must be done to prevent this. The cycad palms and all the knowledge associated with them are part of the Songlines.

A hunter-gatherer lifestyle in Western thought has usually been associated with nomads who wandered aimlessly over the country and chanced upon food. In Aboriginal cultures, nothing could be further from the truth. In every Australian environment there are hundreds of plant species, but constantly testing those plants would be an unfeasible waste of time. Women are the gatherers and men the hunters in Aboriginal society, but these acts involve sophisticated land management. The old 'hunter-gatherer' descriptor is now being recast by writers such as Bill Gammage and Bruce Pascoe to acknowledge such sophisticated practices.[4] However, opinion is divided over use of the term. Some writers, such as Pascoe, choose instead to describe Aboriginal people as 'farmers'.

It is mostly women who harvest and who must have a readily accessible mental record of the hundreds of local plants so they can identify those that are edible, those that are poisonous and those that have other uses, such as medicinal. But they must also know about plants that have been tried and found to be of no use for daily survival. For every useful plant, there are a swag of potential applications to be explored. For example, Anangu people use the many different parts of a *wanari* (mulga) tree to ensure that no resource goes to waste:

Each part of the *wanari* (mulga) tree has an important traditional use.

The heavy, hard wood is the main source of firewood for cooking and smoking meat.

The tree's larger branches and trunk can be carved into *miru* (spear throwers), *mukulpa* (barbs), *wata* (spearheads), *kali* (boomerangs) and *wana* (digging sticks). The leafy branches were used to build *wiltja* (shelters) and *yuu* (windbreaks).[5]

Plants are also an indispensable component of the medical kitbag. Medicines can be made from bark and stems, roots and leaves of trees; minerals in the mud and clay can also heal. Aboriginal healers have specialised knowledge of ways to treat a wide variety of ailments: toothaches, cramps and coughs, headaches and rashes, and wounds from falls and battles. They learn ways to bind breaks and soothe burns, and how a spider's web can stem the flow of blood. They must know which creatures bite and which sting, and how to treat those wounds. They need to know how to prepare plant medicines to ease all the diseases that might afflict their community.

STORIES FROM SO VERY LONG AGO

This information is in constant use. That it is accurately retained for each generation is impressive indeed. But now consider that there is information stored in the Songlines that dates back tens of thousands of years but has no apparent practical use today. Aboriginal people have been telling anthropologists that they know about events from the distant past, but it is only recently that Western science has caught up and been able to confirm the stories and acknowledge that non-Aboriginal people should have been listening far more attentively for the few hundred years since colonisation.

The belief system maintained through stories from Tasmania closely relates to those from the mainland, yet the two populations have been separated since the end of the last ice age, at least 13,000 years ago. For around 500 generations, that knowledge has been kept relatively intact.

Given the importance of Songlines as touchstones for knowledge, it should be no surprise that stories about changes in the landscape are among the most ancient. These stories long predate Western science's understanding of these changes. For example, a

Dyirbal story from northern Queensland tells of how it was once possible to walk to nearby islands such as Palm and Hinchinbrook. Geographers have since concluded that the sea level was low enough for this to be the case at the peak of the last ice age, around 20,000 years ago. The Dyirbal live in rainforest but their story describes a very different terrain. Scientists were surprised to discover that the rainforest in that area is only about 7600 years old – but the Dyirbal were not surprised.

The Victorian Boon wurrung and Kurnai people talk about the landforms in Port Phillip Bay and the path of the Yarra River that flows into it. Evidence they gave to the Select Committee of the Legislative Council on Aborigines in 1858 included details that correlate with recent scientific mapping of the bay floor. Many researchers consider that the bay was last dry at the end of the last ice age, while some claim that it possibly dried out again about 1000 years ago. Both views represent accurate details held in the stories for a very long time.

Geographer Patrick Nunn relates many such examples in his book *The Edge of Memory*.[6] Many of the stories relate to the change in the shoreline as recorded by Indigenous inhabitants of the area. Nunn details twenty-one groups of stories that recall the drowning of the Australian coast. Despite being from different language groups whose speakers lived far apart, the stories all report that people witnessed the coastline being much further out to sea than it is today. They talk about a time when islands now offshore were part of the mainland, and about inhabited landscapes that are now under the waves.

Due to the size of the continent and the distances between its inhabitants, Nunn argues convincingly that these must be independent eyewitness accounts of events that happened over 7000 years ago. He acknowledges the extraordinary feat of passing on this information so accurately in oral tradition from generation to generation more than 350 times:

> Given that people arrived in Australia around 65,000 years ago, tens of thousands of years before the culmination of the last great ice age about 20,000 years ago, we know for certain that they witnessed the subsequent rise of sea level that trimmed back the extremities of their land so swiftly and by such extraordinary amounts. It has been estimated that people living ten millennia ago on the low-lying coastal plain south of the Nullarbor Desert would have witnessed the shoreline moving landwards at a rate of a metre (3¼ ft) each week. And off the northern shores of modern Australia, it has been calculated that during more rapid periods of postglacial sea-level rise, people would have seen the shoreline retreat landwards by 5 km (3 miles) every year – a startling thing to contemplate.
>
> [I]t seems indisputable that some groups – perhaps more than twenty of them – were able to effectively transmit drowning stories across a vast slice of time, making their people the greatest of all the oral chroniclers of human history.[7]

Nunn also collected stories of volcanic eruptions and traced their origins, offering another insight into the longevity and accuracy of Aboriginal stories. Australia is an extremely old continent geologically speaking, which means that volcanic eruptions are now rare. Hence, accounts of volcanic eruptions can be linked to specific events in a way that can't be achieved in areas where eruptions are common and the volcanoes still active.

The Gunditjmara have stories about the Victorian mountain Budj Bim, also known as Mount Eccles. A lava flow from Budj Bim that was thousands of years old was used by Gunditjmara people to construct their renowned system of eel traps, which is now on the UNESCO World Heritage List. The accounts tell of the eruption of Budj Bim. Taking the date of the most recent eruption, the stories are at least 10,500 years old – but new research has suggested that they may date the formation of the mountain to about 37,000 years ago. Supporting this argument, a stone axe was found beneath the rocks from the original eruption, indicating that people were in the region at the time. If this is the case, it is the oldest story in the world.

In South Australia, spectacularly explosive eruptions at Mount Gambier produced four craters. Indigenous stories of these eruptions must be at least 4300 years old, assuming they only date to the time of the most recent volcanic event.

The Gugu Badhun people of northern Queensland describe the way watercourses once caught fire. They also tell of people becoming disoriented and dying as a result of a 'witch doctor' who made a huge pit in the ground. These stories relate to the eruption of Kinrara, one of the youngest volcanoes in Australia, which may have occurred 7000 years ago. The lava flows ran down the river valleys for tens of kilometres and the eruption would have spewed clouds of poisonous gas in ash-rich dust from a crater. This 'witch doctor's pit' would have led to the deaths of numerous local inhabitants.

A Dyirbal story from the Atherton Tableland in northern Queensland describes a volcanic eruption leading to the formation of three crater lakes: Yidyam (Lake Eacham), Ngimun (Lake Euramoo) and Barany (Lake Barrine) in north-east Queensland. The most recent possible dates for eruptions are around 9130, 15,000 and 17,300 years ago respectively.

It is easy to speculate that these stories were created far more recently because people could see the crater lakes and possibly created explanations for them, but there is clear evidence that this is not the case. In northern Queensland there are also much older crater lakes that date back around 200,000 years, long before the first Aboriginal people reached Australia. Tellingly, there are no Aboriginal stories about eruptions creating those lakes.

The Songlines of Aboriginal people provide an extraordinarily robust suite of mnemonic technologies that enable knowledge contained in stories to be accurately retained over spans of time that only a few decades ago would have been considered impossible.

TRAVELLING THE TRADE ALONG THE SONGLINES

The knowledge from so very long ago, along with its constant revival, is memorised and passed on, but only taught to those who have the right to the stories. They may have this right because of their inherited position within the community, or through earning the right by their behaviour and level of initiation. Some knowledge is taught not only within the local language group: Indigenous Australians share knowledge and teach each other, and travel to small and large gatherings to do so. The Songlines are trade routes along which everything, both physical and intangible, can be traded, including knowledge.

Aboriginal historian and scholar Dale Kerwin quotes many different Aboriginal leaders on travelling their Songlines in his book *Aboriginal Dreaming Paths and Trading Routes*. Isabel Tarrago, a senior Arrernte woman from the Simpson Desert, explained:

> People knew the way by song and where the soaks are. The artworks on the ridges and messages for the traders. The ridgeline was a trade route. Mum would travel and sing songs. I remember my mum going to these places and at some of them she would sing. We are linked by song to people at Borroloola by the Dog Dreaming, the mob there are connected to granny and mum through this song and so am I. We are related across huge distances by extension of this Dreaming and song. The country is the text to be read and song is the means to unravel the text.[8]

One of the many functions of Songlines is to act as an exchange network. For example, engraved pearl shells from the Dampier Peninsula in north-western Australia were traded over 3200 kilometres to the Great Australian Bight on the southern coastline. Food and valuable objects were regularly traded over long distances; so are ceremonies, songs, dances, language and ideas. Anthropologists were astounded when Aboriginal women in

Port Augusta, South Australia, accurately provided details of places in a song series describing Alice Springs, 1200 kilometres away. They were able to trace the trading of the ceremony, songs, stories, dances and art back to Alice Springs via the outback South Australian town of Oodnadatta.[9] Knowledge of far-off places connected through Songlines is hugely valued.

Aboriginal people travel a lot. They renew and create relationships, and socialise at small ceremonies and huge gatherings. They travel for seasonal harvests on land, in rivers or at sea, either seeking or avoiding dominant weather events. Whether it be the harvest of cycads or an abundance of fish or eels, large ceremonies have always been timed to ensure that the hundreds in attendance would be well fed. Aboriginal people travel to maintain their Songlines, renew their knowledge and call up Country, to teach the next generation all they need to know, and to trade ideas. Today, they also just travel to see their relatives. They are in constant motion, as anyone knows who has tried to track someone down in a remote region. A Ganggalidda leader explains:

> We had our domestic trade routes that went north, south, east and west, my people the Ganggalidda traded for oysters, sea turtle and dugong from the north and in return we had goanna and turkey. We went to Normanton for ginger lancewood and heavy wood for spears and clap sticks, we went west to Garawa for spear flints and stuff. And we went south to the Waanyi and we also traded for a stone axe from the Kalkadoons.
>
> We never just traded for goods, trading was a time for sharing of ideas and technology such as the woomera and outrigger canoes

with sails. The didgeridoo started in a small place in Arnhem Land and by the time whites arrived it had spread over half the distance of Australia. There was also a lot of ceremony sharing, of food, of stories, of culture and time together. Trade was a time of catching up both pleasure and business. My mob when travelling would grind up the Mitchell grass and make Johnny cakes out of it.[10]

Just as in Western societies, Aboriginal knowledge is intellectual property, and just like intellectual property in any other society, it can be traded. Kado Muir, a Wangkatha man from Western Australia who is also an anthropologist, explains:

Trading ways are roads or *urda* with Songlines and Dreaming Tracks, and these are the ceremonies. My mob traded in songs, intellectual property, we traded in information technologies. If you know the songs, water and food resources are easily found.

Mapmaking cartography – our *Yudurra* – is the information superhighway. Along these Dreaming Tracks there were songs, dancers, designs, stories – these all come together as one construct: if you know the stories you can learn. You can learn these in one location and find all the resources needed to travel. Often they are associated with the waterholes. You know the dot paintings with circles here and there and paths in between. Trading was bundled up with a series of ritual, of songs, ceremonies; relationships, stories were the fundamental basis of Aboriginal trade. It is a universe where people know their relationship to the rocks, trees, earth, sky, people and animals. It is based on personal responsibility to everything.[11]

HOW CAN THE KNOWLEDGE BE SO DEEP AND SO SECURE?

What we read in published anthologies of Aboriginal stories are those told to children to start them on a journey to an adult level of understanding. When considered from within the Aboriginal culture, those outside it are the equivalent of children. As with any culture, children need to learn the basics to have a foundation on which to build new knowledge. Children are taken out into Country to get to know the Songlines that will become a map to their knowledge. They understand about memory palaces from the very beginning and learn through the vivid experiences of songs and stories.

Research into many different Aboriginal cultures shows that it takes thirty to forty years to be taught all the knowledge associated with the Songlines. The training involves knowing all the song cycles and associated dances, visiting all the sacred sites, knowing all the sacred objects, and learning all the designs that encode the information to which you are entitled. Authority and power are granted to those who emerge as the knowledge keepers. Throughout this long process, access to knowledge is considered both a right and a privilege. With the knowledge comes responsibilities for the stories, songs, ceremonies, art and, of course, the Songlines themselves.

When teacher John Bradley was living and working in Yanyuwa Country, he experienced a different way of teaching from what he was used to as a non-Indigenous educator. In the book he wrote with the Yanyuwa families, *Singing Saltwater Country: Journey to the Songlines of Carpentaria*, he explained:

This was how the teaching went. Every verse had a commentary – often not a word-for-word translation, as I was looking for; a kujika verse could convey any number of meanings, depending on context. So it was difficult to capture meanings in writing. Some of the kujika verses in this book have taken years to arrive at as meaningful renditions, after immense distillation of many long conversations. And a kujika cannot render meaning without the commentary. Each kujika verse is like a keyhole through which other ways of knowing can be glimpsed, and the commentary becomes the key – only to lead to another keyhole, for which only further teaching will provide the key.

Learning for me, then, was in stories, visiting country, knowing family, seeing ceremonies, and, above all, understanding the connected matrix of all this knowledge. This is what Dinny and Eileen showed me over the days we worked on this first kujika I ever recorded. However, there were times when I sensed they were being careful, restricting information that I should not, or was not yet ready to, know. Even if the kujika were public, there could be layers of meaning embedded in the words that were not to be disclosed.[12]

ROBUST BECAUSE THEY ARE RESTRICTED

The strength of a Songline is affirmed by the singing of the names of the locations along the networks. Each of the names acts as a metaphor for the associated knowledge. The foundation, the skeleton will be the same, but how much of the flesh that has been added to the skeleton is taught to children will depend on their role in the community and their level of initiation into knowledge transfer. It is only by restricting knowledge that the Songlines have been maintained so accurately over such long periods of time.

You may have played the children's game in which players line up and messages are passed by whispering from one to the next. There is often great amusement because the final message can vary greatly from what was first whispered. This inability for oral transmission to stay accurate over even a few minutes is commonly quoted as a reason to doubt knowledge held in oral tradition, but this logic does not hold up when examined critically. Aboriginal people do not whisper their knowledge and then pass it on unchecked. Songs, stories and answers are owned, and the traditional owners will not grant ownership to a person who has not passed all the testing required to demonstrate that they know and understand what they have been taught. The knowledge is restricted only to owners, and ownership comes with responsibility for the knowledge and for the Country that holds that knowledge. Ownership comes with responsibility for the Songlines.

Some knowledge is women's business, and some is men's. Some will be restricted to only a few very senior members who have trained for many years to acquire rights to the knowledge. Whispered information is not easily remembered, but songs, dances and stories linked to the memory palace embedded in the landscape are highly memorable. All Aboriginal cultures, and all Indigenous cultures the world over, restrict knowledge in this way. Oral tradition has nothing in common with whispered information.

But if these memory techniques so closely correlate with the human brain and have been so incredibly robust over thousands of years on the Australian continent, wouldn't you expect them to be manifest elsewhere in the world?

Of course. There may not be any examples as old as those from Australia, but there is certainly no shortage of examples of the same methods emerging independently elsewhere in the world.

7

SONGLINES EMBRACE THE GLOBE

Songlines were once a universal human endeavour, but this has been lost as writing and technology have pervaded our societies. Songlines as a knowledge system enable humans to retain and transmit knowledge and exploit our natural cognitive skills. Song, story, dance and place operate as a powerful combination not used in Western cultures or by Aboriginal people no longer living on Country.

We are all working from the same brain structure, dictated by the same neuroscience. There is so much to learn *from* Indigenous cultures, not just *about* them – and we don't have to give up any of the benefits of writing and technology. It is instructive to consider how different cultures describe their relationship with the landscape.

As Apache singer and medicine man Nick Thompson says, 'White men need paper maps. We have maps in our minds.'[1] What is striking is how much overlap there is with the Aboriginal concept of Songlines.

NATIVE AMERICANS CALL THEM TRAILS

Right across the Americas, Native American trails served to link events in the past to a specific location. The knowledge was performed in ceremonies full of song, dance and dramatic storytelling. For Native Americans, the past is embedded in landscape features, in canyons and lakes, mountains and arroyos, rocks and vacant fields. These features gain multiple layers of significance throughout an Indigenous person's life. Just like in Australia, there are many Native American tribes and each has their unique perspective on their Country.

Anthropologist Keith Basso worked for three decades with the Western Apache, culminating in his book *Wisdom Sits in Places*.[2] He wrote about how the Apache conceive the past as a well-worn trail, first travelled by the founding ancestors and by subsequent generations of Apaches ever since. What matters most to Apaches is *where* events occurred, not when. They describe the principal themes in the knowledge from the ancestors as the endless quest for survival, the critical role of family and community, and the ethical requirements and responsibilities encoded in the knowledge. The Apache complain bitterly that the way their tribal history has been written by Anglo-Americans is dense, boring and not very useful.

What they complain about most is the way that Western-style history, in written documents, does not excite an audience in the way that the past performed in a ceremony in their home territory can do.

Basso mapped nearly 120 square kilometres in and around the community at Cibecue, recording the Western Apache names for 296 locations. The Apache often travel over their lands, calling on each other to relate their travels in detail through the place names. Almost all the place names take the form of descriptive sentences, making locations memorable and easy to visualise. For example, one name translates to 'Water Flows Down on a Succession of Flat Rocks'. These names act as metaphors, so that saying a single place name is effectively quoting an ancestral speech. Basso describes listening to an Apache cowboy who was sitting on a fence talking quietly to himself. For nearly ten minutes, the cowboy recited a list of place names. When Basso asked him about it, he said he 'talked names' all the time. Why? 'I like to. I ride that way in my mind.' Other Apache told Basso that they recite place names 'because those names are good to say' or 'Its name is like a picture'.[3] Every named place has a story, which can take hours to perform. Some narratives are performed only by the knowledge keepers and serve to explain and reaffirm the complex processes of the origin of the world. Other stories tell of historic events and may be much shorter.

One well-known Apache path is a pilgrimage trail that travels to the Bandelier National Monument in New Mexico, where it connects with a trail of the Zuni, one of the neighbouring tribes and a member of the Pueblo language group. Along the trails, which represent ancient migration routes, there are numerous named locations that are often marked with stone cairns or circles, known as 'shrines'. In travelling the pilgrimage trails, physically or through memory, the Pueblo consider themselves to be ritually retracing their ancestors' journeys. They are not just wandering through the landscape: the rituals performed at the shrines along the paths represent high-order meanings embedded in acts of pilgrimage. The pilgrimage trail from the Bandelier National Monument goes for hundreds of kilometres to a Zuni village, and the list of shrines along the route is considered restricted knowledge. Their names are still recited in Zuni narratives by those who have been initiated to a level where they have the right to perform the stories.

A member of another Pueblo language group, the Tewa, notes that the ancestors are always present for the Pueblo. Although the description of the landscape traversed is usually of a single pathway, the entire landscape is a mesh of trails: 'Spirit pathways, used by both spirit and worshippers, crisscross the entire area.'[4]

SONGLINES ON PACIFIC ISLANDS

The huge Pacific Ocean is dotted with numerous island nations, many of which are inhabited by Indigenous people who maintain their oral traditions. On the east coast of New Guinea are the Trobriand Islands, an archipelago of coral atolls covering around 450 square kilometres. Here, the landscape is used as an index to the song-poetry that underpins the oral tradition.

Many stories from the Trobriand Islands talk about the variations in crop fertility on the different islands and the appropriate agriculture for each. However, one of the most famous stories tells of a flying canoe. It takes place at Monikiniki on the island of Kitava, isolated from villages. Embedded within the story are the instructions needed to make a canoe, including the materials, technology, procedure and social organisation. The story is fixed in the landscape, grounding it so that it cannot be lost, but it can also be adapted as canoe technology improves. Senior Trobriand Islanders wanting to build a canoe are able to mentally dash through all the locations of their secret geography and locate the site at Monikiniki to retrieve the instructions they need. Their landscape is an encyclopedia that holds exactly the information needed to survive in their Pacific Island environment. By locating the story in this one place, changes in knowledge about canoes will not impact all the other stories stored across the landscape and various islands.

This practice of making independent stories part of an indexed landscape allows new ideas to be absorbed without the overall corpus becoming corrupted. This is one of the great strengths of knowledge structured within oral tradition, enabling the structure to survive for long periods of time.

In the southern Pacific Ocean, Rarotonga is the most populous of the Cook Islands (known in Māori as *Kūki 'Āirani*). Rarotonga is only 11 kilometres long and 6 kilometres wide, with deep valleys surrounded by a coastal plain. The oral tradition tells how Tangi'ia Nui fled from Tahiti, and from his eldest brother, to land on Rarotonga. He built a *marae*, which usually consists of at least one carved building and its surrounds. Tangi'ia Nui then proceeded around the island, building forty-six further structures. He left all the marae to the charge of guardians, establishing the ancestors of the subsequent chiefs and priests for the new colony. As he travelled around Rarotonga, he effectively divided the physical landscape and established the marae system as well as the political land tenure system based on the locations of the marae.

The great road on the island, the Ara Metua, replicates the route of Tangi'ia Nui. Before European contact, it was structured and restructured over time to serve as a landscape set of mnemonic locations. It served as a road for people to exchange goods and information and for processions to visit the marae along it. The repetition of the ritual encoded the oral tradition and ensured that it was integrated into daily life. The Ara Metua was the Rarotongan Songline, designed to fit a landscape on a very different scale from the wide spaces of Australia.

The marae on many other Pacific islands are still in use, although sadly not on Rarotonga.

SONGLINES AND WORKING IRON IN AFRICA

In Africa, the Haya, a Bantu-speaking people from north-western Tanzania, are famous for their ability to chant extremely long and complex genealogies. For a long time, it was thought that the Haya used no mnemonic technologies, but eventually it was recognised that anthropologists had not understood the depth of the relationship the people have with their physical environment. They use both natural and constructed features within their landscape to form Songlines for their complex oral tradition, adapting their memory techniques to a settled landscape associating their oral tradition with fields, cliffs, valleys, trees, streams and even crossroads. This knowledge system integrates ideas about religion, the world, Haya history and the origin of Haya villages.

The Haya are ironworkers, and their oral tradition talks about the ancestor who founded the industry, Rugomora Mahe. The stories refer to a massive ficus tree, the Kaiija shrine tree, which, the Haya say, marks the exact location where the first ironworkers built an iron tower so tall that it reached to the sky. Archaeologists originally doubted that African oral tradition was either ancient or accurate enough to indicate such a specific site. However, when they finally excavated, they found the ancient forge exactly as described. The Kaiija shrine tree sits at the exact location. The shock came when the remains of the site were dated to before 500 BCE.

Here it gets a little confusing. King Rugomora Mahe ruled the area around 1675 CE. When he took control of the area, he enclosed the sacred ficus tree within his new palace grounds and then named himself as the founder of the ironworks, the one who had long been referred to in the Indigenous stories. Although these stories told of a much earlier time, no one was sure how long ago. It is now known that the legend of Rugomora Mahe dates to about 1200 years before he was born. The oral tradition is robust enough to accept change yet still locate an exact site that was used well over 2000 years ago.

The Rugomora Mahe Songline includes a sequence of sexually explicit images associated with locations at the palace site. Many of the songs use human reproduction as a metaphor for iron production. A woman's cycle from menstruation to copulation, gestation and birth, through to a return to fertility is represented in the process. The bawdy smelting songs replicate the rhythms of the sexual act. For the Haya, human fecundity and the power of technological knowledge are intricately linked.

Adding a new technology to an ancient oral tradition demonstrates just how flexible knowledge systems grounded in the physical environment can be. The way the Haya incorporated mystical narrative references to encode such a pragmatic process is a dramatic example of the adaptability of Indigenous knowledge techniques and their potential for all humans.

Due to colonisation, most Haya traditions are no longer practised. The Haya, like so many Indigenous Africans, were captured for the slave trade. Dragged away from their landscape, they lost their freedom, their human rights and many of their precious memories.

THE INCA CREATED SONGLINES IN A CITY

In South America, there is remarkable evidence about the power of the landscape from one of the most extraordinary cultures the world has seen: the Inca Empire. Unfortunately, the empire was short-lived, and we are dependent on the records of Spanish invaders and subsequent archaeologists to learn of its achievements.

Over an existence of only 300 years, the Inca came to rule the largest pre-Colombian empire in the Americas. The culture emerged around 1200 CE in Peru, and the civilisation eventually grew to about 16,000,000 people in a territory stretching 4000 kilometres from Ecuador down the Andes mountains into Chile. It was the Inca who built one of the most spectacular cities in the world, Machu Picchu. And they did it all without a writing system.

The Inca outshone all the other major civilisations in the Americas of the time, including the literate Aztecs and Maya. They effectively turned their major city, Cusco, into a massive Songline, with their mental picture of it being forty-one imagined pathways, or *ceques*, radiating like the spokes of a wheel from the Temple of the Ancestors in the centre. Along the ceques were more than 340 sacred sites, known as *huacas* in Quechua, the language of the region. These huacas acted as memory locations.

Some of the ceques were physical pathways dividing the land into wedge-shaped political, agricultural and irrigation zones. Each zone was assigned to a specific kinship group. The proportion of ceques that were along actual roads and those that existed as imagined pathways is not known, but the locations were all physical. As the Inca travelled along the ceques, in memory or by walking, each huaca was visited in order. A specific aspect of the knowledge system was associated with each huaca, such as encoded information to do with irrigation, the calendar, spiritual beliefs or rituals. The ceques and their huacas formed a city-sized memory palace.

Spanish priest Bernabé Cobo carefully described every huaca in a detailed chronicle about the ceque system. Some of the huacas were natural landscape features, such as caves, springs, rock formations, river bends, trees or simple landscape locations marked with stones; others were buildings or constructed watercourses. Still others served as astronomical observatories, enabling the Inca to run an effective agricultural calendar based on solar cycles.

One of the most prestigious huacas, Q'enqo Grande, was a built by Inca king Pachacuti Inka Yupanki. Within it, a cave was sculpted out of the limestone. As the summer solstice approached, the sun lit up the cave, illuminating each of a set of steps in order. It is thought that Pachacuti was responsible for a similar effect at Intimachay, a cave at Machu Picchu.

The landscape roads were closely linked to an extremely sophisticated knotted-cord memory device, the *khipu*. This extraordinary device was made from knotted cords, usually of cotton. A primary cord could have any number of pendant cords, which hung vertically when used. Reading the khipu required attention to the colour, texture, spin and ply of the fibres and the direction in which the knots were tied. The knots were tied to represent numbers and calculations such as demographics, tributes, trade data and calendar references as well as recording laws, census data, details of tributes and trade, rituals and songs, genealogies and histories.

Much like the Aboriginal memory sticks discussed in Chapter 9, the khipu were carried by runners to transmit messages across the huge Inca empire. It took years of training to be a khipu specialist or *quipucamayoc*. These specialists were careful to restrict their learning only to members of their profession. The combination of ceques and khipus enabled Inca leaders to memorise and communicate all that was needed to run their massive empire. A class of knowledge specialists were responsible for memorising speeches, history, relationships, laws, rituals, ceremonies and long complex narratives that formed the basis of the Inca oral tradition. The narratives were performed only for the royal elite in gatherings that were either public or restricted.

When the Spanish arrived in Cusco in 1532, the Inca handed over the design of the ceque system to the Spanish chroniclers encoded on a khipu, but the conquistadors destroyed thousands of khipus. The Inca culture could not survive their onslaught.

THE INUIT AND THEIR ICY SONGLINES

Inuit hunters have an ability to navigate vast areas of country, an accomplishment that has astounded anthropologists for centuries. What is particularly tricky for the Inuit is that they need to know the land intimately in hugely variable weather conditions. The topographical details they know so well are visible only in summer months – for a great deal of the year, their territory is covered by seemingly featureless snow or shrouded in the almost permanent darkness of winter. The climate can dramatically change the landscape during their travels, yet they still manage to find their way. Their acutely refined skills have always been an essential element of Inuit culture. They must not only track animals, but ensure that they can return home again across the huge territory. Both the skyscape and landscape are used to ensure safe travel.

The Inuit tried to share their stories as early as first contact, but the missionaries had a different agenda. Typical is a comment from 1767 in *The History of Greenland*, published by the Brethren's Society for the Furtherance of the Gospel Among the Heathen. After quoting a few stories at a very superficial level, a missionary called David Cranz wrote:

But enough of those absurd stories, which indeed none but the weakest heads harbour even in Greenland. Nay it seems to me that the Greenlanders, who have art enough to veil their craftiness with the curtain of stupidity, have often repaid the relations of the Europeans with such romantic tales, to see how far their sense and credulity reaches, or perhaps to make themselves agreeable to them.[5]

Fortunately, some non-Inuit people were more receptive. As early as 1900, anthropologist Franz Boas became deeply impressed by the Baffin Land and Hudson Bay peoples and their detailed knowledge of the environment. He recognised that a key to understanding their worldview was to look at the place names they gave to define their geography. Unfortunately, most of the oral tradition has been lost as the Inuit were almost all converted to Christianity. However, some of the old tradition survived. 'I know some of the words to the dance songs. I have an image of the land and the old way of life when I sing the songs,' reported May Ikhomik Algona of Inuinnait, Irons.[6]

Over the past fifty years, Inuit elders have been recording their remaining oral tradition, mostly in Nunavut Territory, northern Canada. Inuit elder Hubert Amkrualik explained the role of stories:

Stars were well known and they were named so that they could be easily identified whenever it was clear. They were used for directional purposes as well as to tell time ... stars could be remembered by the legends associated with them. The people before us had no writing system so they had legends in order to remember.[7]

131

As with all Indigenous cultures, names enable the Inuit stories to be recalled:

> All the lakes where you can find fish or caribou have names. That is the only way we can travel. The one way we can recognise lakes is by their names. Sometimes we name them on account of their size or because of their shape. The names of places, of camps and lakes, are all important to us; for that is the way we travel – with names. We could go anywhere, even to a strange place, simply because the places are named. That would be how we find our way. It is the way we can find how far we are from camp or from the next camp. Most of the names you come across when you're travelling are very old. Our ancestors named them because that is where they travelled.[8]

Critically, the Inuit language includes extremely precise vocabulary for describing places. Unlike the European explorers, who named Inuit landscapes after their monarchs and friends, the local people named places by describing either the physical location or its environmental significance. More than 7000 Inuit place names are recorded for northern Québec alone. Much Inuit wayfinding is learnt when young hunters are out on dog-sleds with their fathers or other experienced hunters, but the elders bemoan the fact that young hunters today do not know the place names well enough and have a tendency to get lost.

The Inuit talk about navigating by their travelling songs, which name all the places along the routes. Significantly, the routes learnt were not always the most direct, but they were always the fastest.

To an outsider accompanying an Inuit hunter, a route often appeared haphazard, but to those who knew the pathways, they were simply following their ancestors. The stages were marked by named landmarks of hills and lakes, beaches and boulders, islands and river bends. If there was no useful landmark feature, significant places were marked by stone cairns.

Like other Indigenous cultures, deep knowledge of animals and the environment, plants and humans was woven into and integrated in the knowledge system. Time was marked in various ways: the time of the ancestors, the migration of animals, the astronomical cycles, and stages in an individual's life. The past was in the present. The stories were performed, and the most vital and individual storytellers were revered.

Too often people assume that traditional navigation is done only 'by the stars'. The Inuit are able to make periodic adjustments for stars' apparent movements throughout a hunter's travels. Their calculations involve a thorough knowledge of star and constellation positions, adjusted according to seasonal and nocturnal cycles.

But Inuit astronomy was just one of the navigation tools taught through song and legend. For almost half the year, the Inuit can't use the stars due to the extremely long days. Even during the months with a night sky, the stars are frequently obscured by cloud, fog or blowing snow. The Inuit wayfinders made detailed observations of landmarks, sea currents and floating seaweed, cloud formations and movement, atmospheric effects and wind direction. The stories teach them how to interpret the behaviour of animals, from their own sled-dogs to wild creatures such as walruses and birds. What is almost inconceivable is that the Inuit are able to navigate reliably even when the sea ice is constantly moving. Drawing on the knowledge passed on to them through stories, the wayfinders modify their direction allowing for the movement of the ice and how far they have travelled over it.

One of the most impressive examples of Inuit navigation is their understanding of snowdrifts. For up to eight months of the year, both the land and sea ice are blanketed by snow, which often covers familiar landmarks. These are the months when Inuit do the most extensive travel with their dog teams. Many of the soft drifts are ephemeral and change as soon as the next strong wind blows; others take a more permanent form. The Inuit rely most heavily on formations known as *uqalurait* and *qimugjuit,* which are set down by the prevailing west-north-west wind, called the *Uangnaq.* Abraham Ulayuruluk of Amitturmiut explains:

> During a blizzard, the snowfall is usually soft. A type of snow mound, *uluangnaq*, is formed. The (prevailing wind) then erodes the mound, thereby forming an *uqaluruq* – a drift with a tip that resembles a tongue (*uqaq*) – this is pointed and elevated from the ground – *Uqalurait* are formed by the *uangnaq* ...
>
> The *qimugjuit* all face *Uangnaq*, therefore the *uqalurait* also face *Uangnaq*. If you know the direction of your destination but have lost sight of it, or when you no longer know the general direction of your destination, you can use the *qimugjuit* and the *uqalurait* to guide you. These are the snow formations that you observed during the daylight hours and that you noticed were

facing towards the *Uangnaq*. When the visibility is skewed, either through darkness or bad weather, these drifts will be your only available aid.[9]

SONGLINES IN THE OCEAN GUIDE THE PACIFIC NAVIGATORS

Navigating for Pacific Islanders is much more formal than it is for the Inuit, but it enables these seafarers to treat the ocean as if it is the land, crisscrossed by Songlines.

The Indigenous navigators who sail the Pacific, made famous by the 2016 Disney film *Moana*, depend on a highly structured knowledge of complex navigational law. They are able to sail thousands of kilometres of open ocean and are often at sea for weeks at a time. They do it by mapping the ocean as if it were a set of Songlines on land. The memorised paths are referred to as 'sealanes' or 'roads'. The songs and stories encode the 'landmarks' and teach the seafarers how to adapt for wind and current. One Tahitian chant accurately locates the North Pole Star, Polaris – but a sailor would only be able to sight the star after travelling over 1500 kilometres from Tahiti.

Navigational knowledge right across Oceania is restricted, enabling it to be maintained to the degree of accuracy needed for such amazing feats. The few select members who reach the level of navigator are highly respected and powerful members of their communities.

In the 1970s, the first European to report the stories of the navigators from the Micronesian island of Puluwat considered the stories to be bizarre and fantastical. He simply didn't understand the way knowledge systems work in Indigenous cultures. The stories are imagined by the navigators, the *pelu*, as if they are an animal or ancestral hero moving along the ocean path. The memorised course serves as an index to using the stars and physical places in the ocean for navigation, while also forming an interwoven mnemonic for Puluwatese mythology and culture.

The pelu travel between islands with ease. Before taking charge of a double canoe, they spend about thirteen years training, from the age of five, in a navigational school located in a boathouse. Much of the curriculum is taught on land. They study complex mental imaging by manipulating 'charts' made of sticks and shells or just by moving objects on a mat. The memory locations in the ocean are usually represented by shells and may correspond to real islands, reefs and banks, but they may also be locations that exist only in the imagination. The gaps between the real islands may be represented by 'ghost islands' or mythical beasts to ensure there are enough points for reliable navigation. On the long course from Puluwat to Eauripik, for example (some 680 kilometres), the path follows a row of imagined whales. It takes a day to sail from one whale to the next, with each whale being named and teaching the encoded information.

The navigators learn the way swells and wave patterns will feel around every different island or reef they may encounter. They know the angle a swell will make with their vessel's bow depending on the tide and weather conditions. A highly skilled navigator can determine the slightest of wave movements by entering the water and using his scrotum as a hypersensitive detector.

The pelu learn the behaviour of every animal they may encounter. For example, they learn how frigate birds can indicate rough water. They can estimate the distance and direction to islands by sight or by call of the bird species that hug the islands. They are taught a detailed fish taxonomy and knowledge of the behaviour of each species. Every possible ocean indicator serves as a checkpoint as they travel known routes.

The Puluwat curriculum includes a great deal of astronomy. The students learn to name hundreds of stars and to judge the bearings of their canoes by the way navigational stars rise and set on the horizon. The star charts are maintained in memory so the navigator can shift his focus over the course of a night from one rising star to the next. The mental star compasses are used as a set of memory locations for the physical star positions but can be used even if the stars are not visible. The stars also act as a memory aid for a great deal of oral tradition.

The Pacific navigators were also superb explorers, constantly moving beyond known lands to discover new islands. There are around 25,000 islands in the Pacific Ocean, and over thousands of years, the Pacific Islanders colonised more and more of them. In their search for new islands, they would often travel against the prevailing winds. If no island had been encountered when their food had nearly run out, they would turn and use the tailing wind to ensure a rapid trip home. They visited New Zealand a number of times before finally coming equipped to settle. Eventually, in about 1200 CE, they reached Rapa Nui (Easter Island), one of the most remote inhabited islands in the world, 3500 kilometres from Chile.

The nearest inhabited land is over 2000 kilometres away. But they didn't turn up on this remote island by accident, drifting on a raft, as is often depicted in B-grade movies. They arrived with at least two canoes and the supplies needed to start a new colony, as was their practice.

8

SONGLINES IN SEA AND SKY

Ŋuruku miyamanarawu Dhaŋgala aaaaaaaa …
Wana ŋyerrpu miyaman ŋunha marrtji Baŋupaŋu.
Miyaman marrtji Balwarri Nepaway, Maywundjiwuy.

Of that body of water I sing, I sing of the body of water.
The arm of the paddler is knowledgeable, over there is Baŋupaŋu.
I am singing about Balwarri, the whale, Nepaway, the open sea.

– Gay'wu Group of Women[1]

The concept of Songlines in the ocean is not unique to the Pacific navigators. The ancestors of coastal Australian Aboriginal cultures created not only the landscape but also the seascape. Just like the Gay'wu Group of Women of the Yolŋu, their knowledge of the sea is sung.

SONGLINES SPIRAL IN WATER

The Yolŋu Songlines cross both land and water. In north-eastern Arnhem Land in the Northern Territory, Yolŋu Country includes vast coastlines and the sea beyond. Instead of Songlines, some Yolŋu prefer the term 'songspirals', which travel over land, along freshwater rivers, and where the freshwater and saltwater meet. Yolŋu knowledge of water is unrivalled. It is part of the everyday, of everything.

Although the Yolŋu clans share many aspects of their cultures, they are not a single clan. A dozen languages make up the Yolŋu Matha. All Yolŋu speak many of these languages as well as English. And in all those languages, they sing of the land and the sea. As the Gay'wu Group of Women explained in their 2019 book, *Songspirals*:

> Our connections are to the land and to the sea too. Sea is part of Country. We call this Sea Country. We belong to the sea and the sea belongs to us, just as with the land. We don't see any clear distinction between land and sea, rivers and mangroves, earth and sky; they are all connected through relationships. That is the basis of our authority, our land rights and sea rights. One time we sat down and mapped out connections through the songspirals right into and through the Arafura Sea. We wanted to tell *ŋäpaki*, about this, and that became the basis of our Sea Country native title case, which we won in 2008. We sat down and did the *djäma*, the work. So the whales and the knowledge are linked to Sea Country rights.[2]

The songspirals are all connected, from land to sea and for all of time. They represent a map of Country, and continue into the journey taken after death. They also talk of fishing in speedboats: 'Because – and this is important – the everyday is eternal too.'[3]

The songs often reflect the perspective of a paddler as they move in their canoe along the songspirals. The singer becomes the paddler out on the water, no matter where they are singing and even if they have never travelled that songspiral. The paddler is knowledgeable not only of everything to do with the water but also of the names for the sacred places on land, for all the islands. The knowledge tells of all the clans and all the people, and of the animals. The Yolŋu sing of Balwarri, the whale, and Nepaway, the open sea. They travel with the whale, as told by the Gay'wu Group of Women:

We sing whales swimming with their mouths open, scooping water, filtering fish. We have travelled with them, as them. Now we are part of a pod, flipping and jumping, playing and roaming, feeling the water on our skin. As we play, we know the places. We sing Dhawulwulyun, over there, where the whales or the manta rays are feeding, diving with their mouth open, going down. As we sing, we are connecting, remaking, and when we arrive at a place we sing towards the next place, connecting with it, remaking it. Forever.[4]

Throughout Yolŋu stories there is constant reference to detailed knowledge of the movement of water, both freshwater and saltwater and when the two mix. References are made to the fact that the freshwater is drinkable, and to the different species that live in the alternative habitats. The locations of submerged rocks and coral are recorded, along with the behaviour of the water around and above them. The best areas to visit are sung, as are those that are dangerous and should be avoided. Everything about the water is in the songs.

The ocean is a dynamic place. Islands appear and disappear. Indigenous knowledges are famously adaptable yet also record events over hundreds, at times thousands, of years. An island called Teonimenu, close to Ulawa Island in the Solomons archipelago in the south-west Pacific Ocean, disappeared hundreds of years ago. The top of it is now 10 metres below the ocean surface. The Solomon Islands are notorious for earthquakes, which often lead to tsunamis. The stories tell of a cursed place where the water churned around the island until giant waves struck it again and again until the island sank. Stories from neighbouring islands tell of people from Teonimenu who managed to survive. Their descendants are still fishing those waters.[5]

FROM SEA TO SKY

Closer to Australia, the Torres Strait lies between the northern tip of Queensland and southern New Guinea. Torres Strait Islander Country includes 48,000 square kilometres of shallow sea and less than 600 square kilometres of land spread across at least 274 islands, of which only fourteen are permanently inhabited.

The knowledge system of the Torres Strait Islanders meshes their knowledge of Sea Country and Sky Country with all their cultural and survival needs. The Songlines on land and in water are mirrored in the sky. Their astronomy tells of the first arrival on the islands. The most famous of their ancestral navigators, Tagai, is a hero of the sea for all Torres Strait Islanders although his story belongs to one of the two language groups, the Meriam.

Tagai set out on an outrigger canoe voyage with a crew of twelve men. Their lack of fishing success caused him to leave the canoe to search for fish on a nearby reef. In the heat of the day, the waiting crew grew hungry and thirsty. They drank all the water and ate all the food for the voyage. When Tagai returned and found his own provisions gone as well, he was furious. In his rage, he threw his crew into the sea, six at a time. Their images can now be seen in the northern sky, six of them in Usal (the Pleiades star cluster) and six in Utimal (Orion). The constellation named Tagai spans the southern sky, far from his crew. Tagai can be seen standing in his canoe, formed by the stars of Scorpius. His left hand is the constellation known as the Southern Cross, in which he holds a spear. In this way, he permanently indicates south for Islanders navigating the seas. A much-enjoyed fruit that is sometimes called the Cedar Bay cherry (*Eugenia reinwardtiana*) is in his right hand, represented by a group of stars in the constellation Corvus.

Islanders use the various stars and their positions in the sky to inform them of many aspects of daily life, including the best times to plant their gardens and to hunt turtle and dugong, and to predict weather changes such as the arrival of the monsoons and changes in winds. Tagai's story also teaches moral lessons for the Meriam people about the consequences of stealing and the need to share.

Tagai, Usal and Utimal are just a few examples of Torres Strait astronomy knowledge. The shark constellation Baidam is part of the constellation also known as Ursa Major. The appearance of these stars in the north tells the Islanders that it is the start of the sharks' mating season, which is the time to plant banana, sugar cane and sweet potato. The phases of the moon tell the Islanders when it is the best time to fish.

As Torres Strait Islander academic Martin Nakata says, 'We are not just a people of culture. We are also a people of science.'[6] Indigenous astronomy is well recognised as being sophisticated and scientific, stored through the stories and songs associated with the Songlines in the sky. Torres Strait Islander science, like Western science, is based on detailed observation and is used to predict weather conditions, food cycles and a multitude of aspects of the environment. Despite two centuries of colonisation and religious conversion, traditional Islander astronomical knowledge is still integral to everyday life.

A particularly impressive understanding of the subtle variations in the scintillation – that is, twinkling – of the stars comes from the Torres Strait Islanders. The people are often inspired by the beauty of the twinkling, but they also use it for practical purposes. Their detailed observations have led to a deep understanding of scintillation and its implications for weather and seasonal change. Like many other astronomers, Torres Strait Islanders distinguish planets, which don't tend to twinkle, from stars, which do. Elder Alo Tapim explains how Meriam fishers and gardeners know when the season of Kuki is coming:

There are various signs that the seasons change. We see it in trees and gardens, but mainly in the stars. It becomes quite apparent towards the end of the year when you get the very clear skies and hot days because there are no clouds, and the same through the night. And the stars are there very clear and colourful. When they twinkle, it heralds the wind picking up and fishermen capitalise on that – giving them the idea that they will have a good day at sea. Or they can overnight at the reef and come back the next day by observing these stars.

From spring to summer, we get that dry, hot season where there are hardly any clouds in the sky. The word is doldrum, very fine – not a breath of air – it's very still. During the night, when the dew sets in, you see the stars. They're really shining and twinkling. It's a good sign. It heralds the changes in the weather. Instead of the hot dry season, a wet season is coming. Locals always look forward to that. They observe the stars because the gardener is anxious. When is that rain going to come? They observe the stars, the planets, and the path of the sun. They are aware there is dew at night, even though the sun is hot during the day. The dew rolls right into the dry ground, even though the ground may look brittle on top. When a farmer digs down, it is cool and muddy inside, and this is a result of the dew. Dew keeps the soil soft inside. Maybe a baby cicada or something not fully developed is present. By observing that cicada, it is evident the Wet [season] is near. So by observation of the ground, the environment, and the sky at night, the farmer is reassured that the wet, rainy season is coming.[7]

145

Nakata described Indigenous and Western sciences as complementary, saying that 'We need to privilege both [Western science and Indigenous knowledge] in the appropriate context for appropriate purposes' through what he calls the 'cultural interface'.[8] This is what we refer to as the third archive.

Similarly, the Gay'wu Group of Women talk about the relationship between Yolŋu and Western astronomy:

> In Sky Country there are connections too. It is a river, not just a star or a planet with empty space between. The universe is full, full of connections and stories and beings. There are so many stories and they are in relationship with each other. When we sing the stars, we sing about which direction the morning star comes from, which direction the moon comes from, from which place they come and where they go. There are so many layers.
>
> These layers, they are about relationships here on earth too. They are about bringing messages in the right way. They are about *bala ga' lili*, give and take, where the saltwater and freshwater meet. That happens between Yolŋu and Western knowledges too, a mixing and merging, and a negotiation.[9]

The sky is the same for all of us – nothing any culture does can change it. The stars will always rise and set in the same places on the horizon in their annual cycles; the sun and moon will always move in totally predictable ways. Indigenous and non-Indigenous observers have known and used these facts for millennia. They have noticed the relationship between their observations and the seasons, weather, tides, the behaviour of animals and the flowering of plants.

Indigenous stories have also recorded transient celestial phenomena: changing brightness of stars and the passing of comets, eclipses, meteors and cosmic impacts. Australian Aboriginal cultures aligned stone arrangements with cardinal directions as well as the solstices and equinox, such as at the Wurdi Youang stone ring in Victoria.

THE EMU IN THE SKY

Not only are groups of stars named, but the dark spaces between them are used to form characters whose stories are told.

Many Aboriginal language groups across Australia recognise the 'Emu in the Sky', a dark figure stretching across the Milky Way. One such group is the Kamilaroi and Euahlayi peoples from northern and north-western New South Wales. Euahlayi lawman Michael G Anderson explains that for the Kamilaroi and Euahlayi, the Emu is observed as it changes position and from season to season. The changes closely relate to knowledge of both cultural matters and the resources linked to the Emu.[10]

At the end of summer, the head of the Emu is barely visible on the horizon; the body is below and blocked from sight. The head, the long neck and then the body slowly emerge, and after sunset in autumn the full Emu can be seen stretching from the south to the south-east. According to Anderson, it is then that the Kamilaroi and Euahlayi say the Emu is running. It is also at this time that female emus on land chase males during mating season and eggs become available. In the following months in the sky, the legs disappear and the Emu, now male, can be seen sitting on the eggs, as is the unusual habit of this bird on land. By late winter, the neck becomes indistinct in the sky and the body appears just like an emu egg. At this time on earth, the chicks are hatching and the eggs are no longer available to eat. By spring, the bird in the sky is transformed into a featherless Emu, Gawarrgay or Gawarghoo, who travels to waterholes and cares for everything there. By the end of spring, the Milky Way and the Emu within settle at evening to be low on the horizon. The neck and head are difficult to see, and the Emu is believed to be sitting in a waterhole ensuring that all the waterholes in the country have been filled by the winter rains. By late summer, the Emu has become almost invisible on the horizon, having left the waterholes – which is why the waterholes dry up.

Similar relationships between Sky Country and terrestrial events are found right across Australia, always sensitive to the local environment. For example, the Boorong people of south-eastern Australia recognise many constellations and planets within their narratives of sky and land. Marpeankurrk is the personification of the red giant star also known as Alpha Bootis or Arcturus, the most prominent individual star in the winter sky. Narratives talk about the pupae of the wood ant (termite), a protein-rich staple item of diet. Story tells where best to locate the ants; the position of the star tells when to harvest the food.

Learning the stories in the Sky Country starts from childhood. Senior Wardaman elder Bill Yidumduma Harney describes traditional life in Wardaman Country, near Katherine in the Northern Territory:

In the country the landscape, the walking and dark on foot all around the country in the long grass, spearing, hunting, gathering with our Mum and all this but each night where we were going to travel back to the camp otherwise you don't get lost and all the only tell was about a star. How to travel? Follow the star along ... While we were growing up. We only lie on our back and talk about the stars. We talk about emus and kangaroos, the whole and the stars, the turkeys and the willy wagtail, the whole lot, everything up in the star we named them all with Aboriginal names. Anyway we talked about a lot of that ... but we didn't have a watch in those days. We always followed the star for the watch ... Emu, Crocodile, Cat Fish, Eagle Hawk, and all in the sky in one of the stars. The stars and the Milky Way have been moving all around. If you lie on your back in the middle of the night you can see the stars all blinking. They're all talking.[11]

Like many Aboriginal Songlines, the Seven Sisters Songline takes to the sky when the Sisters become the Pleiades star cluster and their pursuer becomes the 'belt' of Orion. Similarly, Harney describes how for the Wardaman, the Songlines on land were mirrored by the Songlines in the sky when the creator spirits moved to the sky:

One day it was all different, when they come down and make up the Creation line songs, because they travelling. When everything become still. They all split up, land, become all the stars ...

The Dreaming Track in the sky! Planets making the pathway! Travelling routes, a pathway you could call it, like a highway! Travelling pathway joins to all different areas, to base place, to camping place, to ceremony place, where the trade routes come in; all this sort of things. The Dreaming Track in the sky, the planets come straight across ... walking trail becomes a pad, then becomes a wagon road, two wheel tracks, then become a highway. That's how they started off, four of them.[12]

THE FIRST ASTRONOMERS

Australian Aboriginal astronomy is a continuous knowledge store almost certainly dating back to the first arrival around 65,000 years ago. Aboriginal people are often considered the first astronomers in the world because of the detail in their observations and the way astronomy is so intricately woven into their oral traditions.

In traditional life, astronomical knowledge is widespread and far more detailed than that of Western society or city-dwelling contemporary Aboriginal people. The knowledge is held within an integrated cultural context. The stars granted significance in the traditions are not necessarily the brightest nor the most obvious. Some valued stars are as faint as magnitude 4 stars, when most observers notice only magnitude 1 and 2 stars. Some star patterns that feature strongly in the tradition are small and fairly obscure clusters. The pattern and their position in the sky may be more important than their prominence.

Unlike in Western astronomy, constellations are not joined dot-to-dot into figures representing characters such as Sagittarius or Capricorn. Instead, groups of stars form a cast of characters whose stories are told in narrative. Collectively, the narratives form a complex system that makes reference to many aspects of Aboriginal life and law. It creates a calendar linking celestial events, weather conditions and availability of food sources over the annual cycle, but also relates to social obligations, trade meetings and ceremonial obligations. Aboriginal observation was so sophisticated that stories from many coastal areas, such as Yirrkala in Arnhem Land and on Groote Eylandt, demonstrate detailed observation of the cycles of the moon and tell of the relationship between the phases of the moon and the tides. For example, 'When the moon is new or full and sets at sunset or sunrise respectively, the tides are high; when the moon is in the zenith at sunrise or sunset, the tides are low.'[13]

In Western cultures, astronomy is a discrete discipline, but for Aboriginal people, astronomy is an inherent aspect of cultural life. The dramas played out on the ground and in the sky articulate far more than the availability of resources or movement of the tides. They tell of the human condition, of good and evil, of laws and expectations, of ceremonies and totems.

THE SEVEN SISTERS TAKE TO THE SKY

Putuparri Tom Lawford, a Kimberley Wangkatjungka man, said in 2007, '*Kartiya* law is all written down on paper: Blackfella law is written in the stars, on the ground, on the Countryside, in the hills, everywhere.'[14]

The Seven Sisters Songline is also written on the ground and in the stars. At Kuru Ala in the Great Victoria Desert, the story becomes sinister. Wati Nyiru's obsession with the eldest sister culminates in his capturing her, then leaving her ill and weak after her ordeal at his hands. It is here that the sisters take to the sky and become the seven stars of the Pleiades cluster. Wati Nyiru continues to pursue them and can be seen as the 'belt' of the Orion constellation – but, given his lustful intent, the belt is interpreted as a sexual organ. The mnemonic for the Seven Sisters saga is no longer the surrounding topography. It is now the night sky: the Orion constellation and Pleiades star cluster canopied above. The story of the Seven Sisters never ends. Their journey will always be happening, in the features of the land and, each night, in the sky. And as we know, their story is also powerfully told in art.

9

ART IS CULTURE MADE VISIBLE

From the earliest days of Aboriginal cultures, as will be the case forever, art has been an integral component of the knowledge system. Songlines are often represented, calling up Country with every representation. A contemporary example is *Kungkarangkalpa – Seven Sisters* (2015) by the Ken family, held in the collection of the National Museum of Australia.

TJUKURPA LIVES IN OUR MINDS

Tjungkara Ken, the youngest of five sisters, dreamed about painting on a round canvas. Her sisters were delighted when they were asked to participate in it: Yaritji Young drew the outline showing the journey

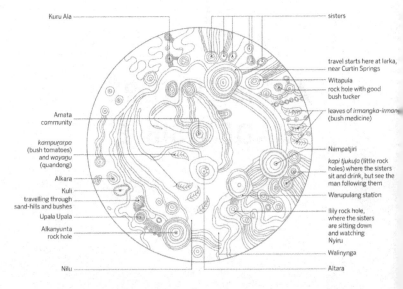

Kuru Ala

sisters

travel starts here at Iarka, near Curtin Springs

Witapula

rock hole with good bush tucker

leaves of *irmangka-irmangka* (bush medicine)

Amata community

kampurarpa (bush tomatoes) and *wayanu* (quandong)

Nampatjiri

kapi tjukula (little rock holes) where the sisters sit and drink, but see the man following them

Alkara

Kuli

travelling through sand-hills and bushes

Warupulang station

Ilily rock hole, where the sisters are sitting down and watching Nyiru

Upala Upala

Alkanyunta rock hole

Walinynga

Nilu

Altara

Diagram of *Kungkarangkalpa – Seven Sisters*

Irawa Bore

Angas Downs

Curtin Springs

Iarka (salt lake)

Aniri — Atila (Mount Conner)

Witapula

No.3 Bore

Mulga Park station

Walinynga (Cave Hill)

Kuli

Alkara

○ Seven Sisters sites
--- where they flew
● other locations

Diagram of the Anangu Pitjantjatjara Yankunytjatjara (APY) Seven Sisters Songline

154

of the Seven Sisters from Iarka through the Ken family's country to Kuru Ala. The resulting painting attracted a lot of attention from her fellow artists. As described in the *Songlines* exhibition catalogue:

The Seven Sisters are depicted as seven circles at the top of the canvas. They crossed the salt lake, Iarka, which is near Curtin Springs, and walked to Witapula, a rock hole, where they swam. Frightened by Wati Nyiru, who had followed them, the sisters dived into the water and swam underground to emerge again at No. 3 Bore. Here they found good bush foods and also *irmangka-irmangka* (poverty bush), a plant with strong-smelling leaves from which they made bush medicine for rubbing onto their sore body parts. Always followed by Wati Nyiru, the sisters walked to Nampatjiri and then to Kapi Tjukula (which means 'rock holes'), where they sat down and drank water. They saw the old man following them and they pushed on to Warupulang, the old cattle station, and then to Ilily, another rock hole where they rested and observed Wati Nyiru. They continued on to Altara and then to Walinynga, where they made a shelter that turned into a cave, painted to this day with beautiful rock art designs. From here the sisters walked to Alkanyunta, a big rock hole filled with water. They found *kampurarpa* (bush tomatoes) and *wayanu* (quandong). The sisters crossed sandhills and walked through bushes to Upala Upala, and via Kuli to Alkara. Nearly 600 kilometres into their journey, the sisters finally arrived in Kuru Ala, an important Seven Sisters site.[1]

When senior Anangu woman and artist, custodian and healer Rene Kulitja says, 'Art learns us',[2] she means that art, as in painting, is like song, story and performance – another way to learn culture, to learn your Dreaming, your Tjukurpa. Painting for Anangu is never primarily about expressing a personal emotion as it is likely to be for a Western artist. Nor is a painting a realistic representation of a scene or object. It won't be an appealing view of nature such as you might see in the works of Rex Batterbee, the Western artist who taught the famous Aboriginal artist Albert Namatjira to paint watercolour landscapes. Aboriginal and Torres Strait artists can only paint or make things on subjects that they are entitled to. That is, they paint their Dreaming and their Country and the myriad topics within. They cannot paint someone else's story or Country. So while Namatjira's watercolour landscapes look to all intents and purposes like Batterbee's, Namatjira is only painting his Country, and all the marks on that Country are cues to the Dreaming stories.

Most contemporary Aboriginal art is done for non-Indigenous audiences using Western materials. It functions like a passport between cultures enabling cross-cultural access to knowledge that has been scripted into the work.

ART IS COUNTRY

Wherever the ancestors went, they left a trail in the landscape that is not only physically visible on Country but experienced through the songs, dances and art originally created by the ancestors. It is embodied in these various art forms. Australian Indigenous art is Country. It provides a map of the land – every significant feature was once known and mapped – but this map is not cartographic. It is not analogous to a Western map that has a fixed scale and a conventional orientation. An Indigenous painting may have multiple orientations and is often painted by a group of artists seated around it on the ground.

To consider a piece of Indigenous art as simply a map would be so superficial as to lose most of the intent behind it. Indigenous art is a system of knowledge that includes mapping the landscape but also makes reference, always, to the way the landscape is to be understood in terms of the stories and teachings of the ancestors. Country is the connective tissue; kinship between people, place and paintings is inseparable.

Art conveys intellectual knowledge. It may also be beautiful, but the aesthetic is integrated with the intellectual. In *Saltwater: Yirrkala Bark Paintings of Sea Country*, Aboriginal curator Djon Mundine writes: 'Aboriginal bark paintings are more than just ochres on bark: they represent a social history; an encyclopaedia of the environment; a place; a site; a season; a being; a song; a dance; a ritual; an ancestral story and a personal history.'[3]

From caves to cliffs, from wood to textiles, art serves as a mnemonic device. Paintings also have a political purpose, representing the rights of individuals and their association with moieties and clans. Artworks are spiritually powerful designs owned by clans to recall ancestral events. Aboriginal research fellow Dr Dale Kerwin considers Aboriginal art to be writing:

Aboriginal writing is holistic, because corroborees, paintings drawn in the dirt, etchings on bark, wood, or rock, and body paintings are all systems of writing. They carry a message and are tangible and independent of vocals. The message is conveyed as structured and follows set rules, which are dictated and taught by the Elders of a community.[4]

In many cultures, such as the Yolŋu cultures of Arnhem Land, the process of creating a painting is the prime purpose. It is a form of mediation with the ancestors, a visual means of reconnecting with Country, an affirmation of identity or a way of teaching others. The final product may be destroyed or buried or left to decay naturally. Traditionally, these paintings are often collaborations. They may be produced on a flat surface, such as a sheet of bark, or on an object such as a hollow log coffin or a grave post from the Tiwi Islands. A collection of clanspeople with rights to the story and clan design will execute the work for a ceremony or another event of significance. While each person holds a different part of the story, working collectively reinforces kin relationships with others and with the land.

The hollow log coffins you see in art installations at galleries and museums have not been used for funerary rites but have been produced as artworks to be sold in the Western art world. Hollow log coffins are often richly decorated. When the funerary rites are completed, which can take a number of years, the deceased has been properly sent back to his or her ancestral realm. There is then no further use for the coffin, which contains the bones of the deceased. It stands in the camp and is no longer attended.

Artist and filmmaker Lynette Wallworth collaborated with the Martu artists from the Pilbara region in Western Australia in 2013 for an epic 3 metre × 5 metre painting on Country. The painting, *Yarrkalpa (Hunting Ground)*, discussed in Chapter 3, replicates the landscape around Parnngurr, showing the ranges, grassland, gullies, spinifex, sandhills, sand plains, creeks, rocky hills and watercourses, claypans, soaks and fire scars from cultural burning. Specific plant species are linked to their appropriate habitat. Critically, the painting incorporates the embodied knowledge of each of the artists who painted their own tract of Country on different sections of the work, but it all comes together seamlessly on the finished canvas. It also replicates the way the knowledge system works. All the segments, owned by different clans and individuals, come together to create the whole. Each artist contributes their knowledge of places, memories, ancestors, seasons, resources, hunting and living.

The experience had a huge impact on Wallworth:

When we travel back across the country I feel as though I am moving across the painting, as though I am small, and the expanse around me has become more distinctive, because of the painting. I look at the colours across the land and realise that, because of the painting, I am seeing definition in bushes and plants and sand that I had missed before.[5]

ABSTRACT ELEMENTS OFFER A MULTIPLICITY
OF MEANINGS

If you look at Aboriginal art, you soon notice that much of it is abstract, not representing immediately identifiable animals or people. This is one of the strengths of Indigenous art as an integral part of the knowledge system. An abstract design might represent an animal, or its tracks, burrows, nests or behaviour, and therefore ways to hunt a mammal, capture a lizard or dig up a nest of honey ants. It may also represent an ancestor.

Even within a single artwork, the abstract design elements may encode a multiplicity of meanings depending on the context and the viewer's level of knowledge. A circle is easy to identify in shape, and invariably denotes a site of significance. It may represent a camp site, a waterhole, a camp fire, a feature of Country or a sacred place on the Songline. It might represent all of these at once. There will be restricted levels of knowledge associated with the circle so that in any given work only those with the appropriate status will know the other layers of meaning.

The layers of meaning built into abstract or symbolic designs constitute a highly adaptable knowledge system. It is this adaptability that has enabled Aboriginal people to record their knowledge over vast distances and widely varying environments within their own tribal tract of Country. Even more impressive is the way Aboriginal people have adapted their knowledge system to varying conditions, from sea-level rises to habitat variability and contact with other peoples, Indigenous or otherwise. If their art was purely representational, a great deal less could be included in a single work. By using abstract symbols, multiple meanings can be associated with them and 'written' into a painting or engraving.

THE PERMANENCY, YET ADAPTABILITY, OF ROCK ART

Walinynga, also known as Cave Hill, is one of the most magnificent rock art sites in Australia. It is a natural monument in Pitjantjatjara territory, South Australia, 40 kilometres from the Northern Territory border. Walinynga is the only known rock art site for the Seven Sisters Songline. The paintings in the cave also feature a number of other Songlines that traverse the Anangu Pitjantjatjara Yankunytjatjara (APY) Lands at that place.

The art tells stories as ancient as the land itself and as present as the latest adaptation, its meaning relevant for the forever future. The rock reveals just one of the many layers of complexity in the story of the Seven Sisters.

The main traditional owner of the site, Stanley Douglas, defends Wati Nyiru, insisting that he wanted to approach the sisters in the 'proper way' when they were trapped in the cave. His *malpa*, which Douglas politely calls Wati Nyiru's 'special friend', got so excited at the possibility of making the sisters his wives that he lost control, sparking the timeless pursuit along the Songlines. His malpa grew so long that he needed to wrap it around his waist. At one stage, that unruly member struck the rock and created a long groove that can still be seen. The sisters eluded him yet again, rushing through an opening at the back of the cave. Outside, they danced their escape and fled. The story leaves Walinynga but in the cave it is still told.

If you lie down in the cave, you can observe images thousands of years old, including abstract designs, numerous human figures and a host of animals. This experience was replicated in the projection dome theatre at the *Songlines* exhibition at the National Museum of Australia. Visitors to the exhibition could lie beneath the dome and watch vision of Country, including Walinynga, while hearing Aboriginal voices tell the stories of the Seven Sisters amid ambient sounds of Country. These teachings were brought to life by the fire and torchlight illuminating the art. Does Walinynga actually represent one of the first cinematic experiences created on earth?

In among all the animals are extremely accurate renditions of horses and camels, symbolising Indigenous adaptability to the new knowledge that came with colonisation and contact with other cultures. The appearance of these introduced species helps to date different sections of the art. Adaptability is also evident in the adjacent community, Amata, which is home to artists who are active participants in the global art market. Today, Indigenous work from most art centres in remote regions is recognised by major galleries and awards. In 2019, Sylvia Ken from the Amata community won the prestigious Art Gallery of New South Wales Wynne Prize for landscape painting with a work entitled *Seven Sisters*. The Seven Sisters Songline continues to live on through the contemporary art movement, offering more layers of complexity than anyone can ever fully know.

Aboriginal rock art isn't simple, unchanging or static. Artists sometimes superimpose new paintings over old as part of ceremony. Far from being disrespectful, the act of overpainting is one of revitalisation, respect and renewed engagement with all that the art, songs, stories and Country mean.

At Walinynga, a series of concentric circles and tracks were painted over as recently as 1974 – but not for the purpose of renewal. Those circles and tracks had to be painted over to obscure them from outsiders and the uninitiated as the symbols could be too powerful and dangerous for them. Given that the cave now attracts non-Aboriginal tourists, they were painted over to protect outsiders and the uninitiated from potential harm. This demonstrates the cultural sensitivity about vulnerable people being exposed to restricted knowledge.

ROCK ART ACROSS THE WIDE LAND

All over the continent, rock art sites record knowledge both public and restricted, functioning like history books of the continent. They highlight continual adaptation to environmental changes and climatic conditions and record responses to relatively recent contact from outside – some welcome, some much less so. It is art that gives us evidence for the claim that Australian Aboriginal cultures represent the oldest continuous culture on earth.

Abstract geometric symbols and images of animals and tracks date back to the earliest art. If an image was created with red ochre, then it is particularly durable. Images made with white clay are less so; hence, what we read into the art record must reflect the fact that some parts have survived and others are surely gone. What we look at in the most ancient art is only a partial record of what has been painted, yet it still tells a very old story.

Anthropologist Howard Morphy, who works closely with Aboriginal cultures in Arnhem Land, considers the artwork in western Arnhem Land around Gunbalanya – formerly called Oenpelli – to be the oldest, most continuous and most complete art record anywhere in the world. Demonstrating that Aboriginal culture is dynamic and adaptable, the art morphs through a sequence of styles, reflecting tremendous transformation over time. The landscape around the Alligator Rivers region, where they were painted, constantly changed. Around 15,000 years ago, before the end of the last ice age, it was far inland. Australia was still connected to New Guinea, and the Gulf of Carpentaria had not yet been inundated. In the arid region the population was sparse, so there are few rock art sites dating from this very early stage and the paintings at these sites reflect an inland environment. The earliest images, which are of hand-stencils and animals, survive because of their red ochre foundation. There are kangaroos and wallabies but no saltwater species. There are images of boomerangs that disappear when the forest becomes denser and boomerangs are less effective. Around 10,000 years ago, dynamic figures appeared – graceful, energetic and often adorned with headdresses, weapons or other objects, such as goose-feather fans. The images are finely detailed and show hunting, fighting or ceremonies. Later again, the Rainbow Serpent is depicted for the first time. As the region's environment was stabilising, the vegetation began to reflect a greater diversity. Morphy describes the past few thousand years as a time when the freshwater flood plains emerged as an abundantly rich environment offering a seasonally varying smorgasbord of fish and wildfowl, along with vegetables including tubers and rush corms. Knowledge systems will always reflect the transformation of the environment, with the art styles gradually changing over the past 3,000 years to the contemporary western Arnhem Land motifs. Although many themes remained constant, such as human and animal scenes, it is during this time that the distinctive and evocative 'x-ray art' emerged to become the dominant feature. The details of the internal organs and bone structures of animals had previously been depicted, but the style became the defining characteristic of the imagery. These depictions provided a wonderful teaching tool within an aesthetically stunning style of art. It is the duration of the art styles, ever changing, ever evolving, that provides the evidence of a dynamic but continuous culture.[6]

For hundreds of years, Macassan sailors visited from South Sulawesi in Indonesia during the wet season to collect and process sea cucumbers (trepang), which they would trade with the Chinese. The visitors arrived on fleets of thirty to sixty boats known as *praus*, and Aboriginal artists captured the events by painting the praus on rock shelters around the Gunbalanya region and on Groote Eylandt. The visitors apparently were welcomed and respected the local culture. They, unlike the British, were temporary: they came and went. Their visits continued until they were banned in 1906 by the Australian Government.

The British came to stay and colonise, but these visitors were far less respectful than the Macassans. Around Australia, the arrival of Europeans is also represented. There are detailed engravings of their ships on the rocks around the Hawkesbury region near Sydney, probably dating to the arrival of the First Fleet, and their wagons were engraved into the rocks south of Arnhem Land as they progressed north. The X-ray artists of western Arnhem Land recorded horses, buffaloes, boats stacked with cargo, guns and attire.

ABORIGINAL ART IN ALL ITS FORMS

Aboriginal mark-making is now usually referred to as 'art'. That term can often be interpreted as objects appreciated for their aesthetic qualities only, but that is never the case with Aboriginal art. It can take a wide variety of forms, painted in caves and on rock, bark and bodies. It may include masks and headdresses, decorated posts, figurines, memory boards, notched staves, batik, motifs on shields, boomerangs and food dishes, knotted cords, dillybags, sets of objects, wood carvings, sculptures and ephemeral drawings in the sand. Morphy describes the importance of art as a part of major ceremonies. The performances were relatively infrequent, often associated with rituals relating to initiation, death or fertility. Sacred names were incanted and ancient stories enacted. Morphy details the immense scale of these undertakings, a theatrical performance in which the performers take on the ancestral form by painting their bodies, enhancing their masks and elaborate headdresses. The hugely varied creative forms integrated within the event all originated in the ancestral past. The result is a coordinated performance involving song, story and dance, along with painting, sculpture and the art of costume. The particular ancestor invoked is the originator of the song being sung and also the associated designs.[7]

Art is such an integral part of Aboriginal life that it appears in almost every context imaginable. If there is going to be a gathering, then people need to know when and where to turn up. One way they could find out was via message sticks, consisting of lengths of wood, and sometimes bone, marked with a wide variety of geometrical or representational designs. Message sticks were a communication device, a letter, a design for purpose. They were used to summon people to gatherings for corroborees, or meetings of smaller groups for specific events or to resolve disputes, and as notes of introduction to those whose country you needed to cross. They could be inscribed to indicate where to find water, food and shelter and to guide navigation. Acting as a mnemonic device, they were often meaningless without the memory of the bearer.

The Snowy Mountains offered an annual feast in south-eastern Australia. Each spring, millions of bogong moths migrate from their breeding grounds in southern Queensland and go into a state of torpor in the mountains' rock crevices, escaping the heat. They provided a protein-rich food that could be easily collected to feed the sudden influx of people, enabling ceremonies to last for weeks. The exact timing of the migration varies, so the hosts would send out notched message sticks with their emissaries, firstly to prove their credentials and then to inform visitors from a huge area that it was time to come for the corroborees.

Many other decorated objects are far more than practical devices containing artistic designs. For example, spearthrowers can carry information much like message sticks: identity, clan and descriptions of Country can all be inscribed. The guidebook to the Bunjilaka Gallery of the Melbourne Museum emphasises that 'Knowledge is the key that allows objects and the symbols or designs to be read like a map'.[8] On display is a *lankurru* (spearthrower) that was made in 1957 in the Western Desert in Western Australia. Each of the thirty-six circles on it represents a named waterhole. Senior Yolŋu spokeswoman and artist Banduk Marika explains that:

> Knowledge is the key that allows objects and the symbols or designs to be read like a map … The dancing and artwork is your whole life. You have to know your traditional artwork that ties in with the land and ties in with the creation – where your boundary is, how far your ancestor has travelled. It's all written in the art. That is what the traditional art means – owner to the land.[9]

A very different object is the coolamon – a curved, carved food dish. Warlpiri woman Nungarrayi explained the designs on a century-old coolamon from Central Australia:

> The symbols on the coolamon are a 'message stick' and represent messages only known by those who carved them. As coolamons were carried from place to place, the symbols reminded people of meetings, places, stories, events and travels across the landscape's dreaming tracks, in the footsteps of the ancestors and creation

spirits. Such symbols also had levels of meaning according to who read them. Initiated women would know the deeper meanings.[10]

Aboriginal art is as dynamic and evolving as the continuing culture. Ancient traditions and practices inform this living practice. While the rules of ownership and the narrative may be ancient, the tradition is constantly revisited and adapted through contemporary art. For example, the Tjanpi Desert Weavers, formed in 1995, used to make mostly baskets but started to incorporate new materials and techniques into old ways to create contemporary works for different purposes. They wove the well-known almost life-sized realistic Toyota vehicle that won the major award in the Telstra National Aboriginal & Torres Strait Islander Art Award at the Museum and Art Gallery of the Northern Territory in 2005. After that, they were commissioned to make many large-scale artistic creations, including a flying Seven Sisters and a series of trees that morph into the Seven Sisters as they attempt to camouflage themselves to hide from their pursuer. Purchased by the Museum of Contemporary Art in Sydney, the work also includes a soundscape that gives a multi-sensory immersive dimension connecting to both traditional and contemporary art practice.

The Tjanpi Desert Weavers spent three weeks at Kuru Ala to bring part of the Kungkarrangkalpa (Seven Sisters) Tjukurrpa alive for the *Songlines* exhibition, which included a major installation of life-sized *tjanpi* made by the group. The large grass sculptures were based on the traditional grass sculptures originally made from spinifex and other native grasses for domestic use but contained raffia, coloured wool and felt as well as spinifex. Using branches collected and bound together, and wire to provide strength, the weavers created the frames of the sisters; then, with grass and string and wool, the figures took shape, their arms reaching for the sky. The grass was stitched to provide the strength and stability to hold the fingers, breasts, hair and eyes, and the all-important decoration. The sculptures were danced to life – modern art invigorated by ancient choreography.

Some of the most restricted and sacred artefacts are *tjuringa* or *churinga*, which, among other things, act as deeds to land, a representation of Country, along with the responsibilities this implies. To make a tjuringa, skilled carvers inscribe a wide range of ancient geometric designs on a large, flat piece of wood or stone. An elder chants extensive knowledge of Country as he sits with the tjuringa across his knees, tapping each portion of the design as he sings. The designs represent navigational paths, camp sites, animal tracks, plants and totems of the Dreaming stories; and include multiple lines, zigzags, concentric circles, dots, double grooves, U-shapes and animal tracks. Small arcs may represent witchetty grubs, and concentric circles may represent honey ants. All are combined in a sacred and secret design. Senior men store tjuringa on country, often in remote caves. Special 'keeping places' like the Men's Museum at Yuendumu have now been built to securely store tjuringa that had to be brought in from Country as people moved to government settlements.

Some art features on much larger objects. Decorated poles are most famously Native American and Canadian First Peoples' totem poles, where images are presented sequentially up or down the pole, enabling an ordered recall of songs and stories. Intensively decorated poles also play a significant role in Aboriginal sacred life. Some are mortuary poles, signifying the life and Country of someone who has died; others feature as part of ceremonies.

The Yolŋu Djungguwan ceremony in Arnhem Land is performed on a public ceremonial ground where the Wawilak (Wagilag) sisters danced the watercourses as they formed the land and cut down trees to search for precious honey. Ceremonial posts represent both the trees and the sisters themselves. A feather string joining the posts represents the path the women took on Country. Along its length, knots represent important sites on the journey of the sisters along the portion of the Songline being enacted. Designs on the posts also represent different places on the journey as the sisters created Country. The ceremony is performed today as a replication of the ceremony originally performed by the Wawilak sisters in ancestral times. The elaborate ceremonial ground is dismantled afterwards, its presence ephemeral, its purpose served.

Many Aboriginal artforms are ephemeral; they live only in the moment. For example, body painting is a critical aspect of ceremonial life where sacred concepts are painted, the designs depending on the Country to which the people belong and the clan celebrating. The body painting may carry complexity, the meaning at any given time depending on what song is being sung. Afterwards, it is removed.

The ground may bear temporary signs of story. It may not only be danced on, but also painted. A cleared area of sand can become a canvas for drawings done with fingers, possibly with the addition

171

of leaves, twigs or other objects. Sometimes these ground paintings are used like a blackboard in a classroom and wiped clean at the end of the lesson. Figures drawn in the sand can represent a feature of Country or the character of a critical story teaching about everyday life, expectations, ethics and responsibilities. Other times, ground paintings can stretch over 100 metres. Such paintings are produced by members of gathered clans who each contribute their part to the story. In this way they tell of waterholes and camping grounds, groves of trees, events and food eaten on the way. Every aspect of life and Country becomes a symbol on the ground.

In some ceremonies, each scene is erased before the next is produced. The narrator provides a soundtrack as the scene is drawn, sung and then brushed aside. Sometimes the sand paintings are images created by the feet of dancers, the resulting patterns being specific to the ceremony that is being performed.

YOLŊU BARK PAINTINGS RECORD A CHANGING WORLD

In north-east Arnhem Land, Yolŋu artists still paint on bark in the way they always have, keeping the stories and Songlines alive. They start with outlines of the designs, which represent the complex stories and major characters located in their sacred space, then fill the designs with dense cross-hatched lines and block fills. Every detail connects the artist to his or her totemic spirit in Country. The designs have been handed down as sacred property for each clan since ancestral times and serve as title deeds to the land and symbols of political power.

Bark paintings map hundreds of kilometres of the physical and cultural features of the coast, as described by Yolŋu artist Dula Ŋurruwuhun: 'By painting these designs we are telling you our story. From time immemorial we have painted just like you use a pencil to write with. Yes we use our knowledge to paint from the ancient homelands to the bottom of the open ocean.'[11]

But the Yolŋu also have new designs and new priorities as they adapt to the world they share with the many other cultures in modern Australia. They use light boxes and digital art forms and carve patterns into rubber conveyor belts from the dismantled mines at Nhulunbuy in north-east Arnhem Land.

In 1957, leaders of Yolŋu clans demonstrated their integration with the Christian world by deciding to create a set of carved and painted objects near the church on Elcho Island. This demonstrated the unity of the Yolŋu clans and their willingness to negotiate with Europeans, but on Yolŋu terms. In 1962, senior Yolŋu artists painted a pair of monumental panels for the church at Yirrkala – one by the Dhuwa and the other by the Yirritja moiety. When land was excised from the Arnhem Land Reserve, the Yolŋu response was to send a petition on two pieces of bark. Received in parliament in 1963, the typed portion of the bark petition, in Yolŋu and English, was surrounded by sacred designs, one for the Dhuwa and the other for the Yirritja moiety. Australia's Magna Carta, it is now publicly displayed in Parliament House, Canberra.

In 1996, custodian Wäka Mumungurr was inspecting the sacred area of Garraŋali, the ancient home of Bäru, who took both human and crocodile form. His direct descendants are the Madarrpa clan, who have always lived on the shores of Blue Mud Bay. There, Wäka came across the horrifying and distressing debris left by an illegal barramundi fishing camp: among the fuel drums and food scraps was a hessian bag containing the severed head of a crocodile. The preface of the book produced by the Buku-Larrnggay Mulka Centre, *Saltwater: Yirrkala Bark Paintings of Sea Country*, tells what happened next:

> This apparently small incident began the monumental story of the production of 80 bark paintings – set against the backdrop of a national legal and political maelstrom. While these barks were being painted, we saw the historic recognition of Native Title in the sea by the Federal Court one day … and its extinguishment by the Parliament literally two days later. Through all this, the events set in train by Wäka's discovery continued as inexorably as an incoming tide. These works in this catalogue have been brought in by the tide.

> Wäka reported what he found to Djambawa Marawili, Madarrpa clan elder and Chairperson of Buku-Larrnggay Mulka, the Art Centre at Yirrkala. Disgusted and frustrated at the continual invasion of his sacred area and the sacrilege of dismembering of Bäru in his own nest, Djambawa sought to channel those feelings and sat down to paint the sacred designs (miny'tji) of the area in order to educate strangers about the law that Yolŋu live by. He called

a meeting of the elders at Buku-Larrnggay and the artists of the region followed his lead. The rest is history.[12]

In July 2008, the High Court of Australia recognised these paintings as the equivalent of title deeds to the sea rights of the coastal waters of the Blue Mud Bay region. Along with traditional owners of most of the Northern Territory coastline, Yolŋu have exclusive access rights to the tidal waters overlying Aboriginal land. By publishing the artworks in print form, the Yirrkala artists were entering the third archive, combining their ancestral archival techniques with those of the Western archive.

The huge commercial interest in contemporary Indigenous art has meant that Indigenous artists, within their communities, have had to adapt to this new aspect of their lives. Yolŋu artists have also adapted to the commercial art scene, producing large numbers of bark paintings to sell as art, not artefact. These represent a new style that does not reveal the restricted knowledge of 60,000 years of art from the *wangarr*, the ancestral period. Yet again, the Yolŋu have demonstrated their ability to adapt while holding on to their very ancient, and still very contemporary, culture.

THE UNIVERSALITY OF INDIGENOUS ART FORMS

We have the longest art record in the world in Aboriginal Australia. The art forms seen here, however, are found all over the world, albeit implemented in very different ways. The human brain is the common factor in all of them.

Message sticks in various forms are recorded globally. These objects were produced from iron in Africa, and the Māori use carved sticks with multiple knobs beneath a stylised head as mnemonic devices. When reading the Māori *rakau whakapapa*, for example, each knob represents a generation, enabling oral specialists to recite the genealogy and associated knowledge by touching each of the knobs in turn.

Similar in function to the tjuringa were the birch-bark scrolls of the Midewiwin or 'Grand Medicine Society' of the Ojibwe or Chippewa of North America and Canada. Mnemonic motifs were recorded on sacred scrolls fashioned from birch bark and could be read only by those trained within the society. Very few of these scrolls, if any, are produced today. Similar in structure, elaborately carved song boards act as mnemonics for the songs during ceremonies of the Native American Ho-Chunk (formerly known as the Winnebago).

The *lukasa* of the Luba people of the Democratic Republic of the Congo function in the same way. The Luba Bumbudye, or 'men of memory', together formed a powerful, elite and secretive society called the Mbudye. These men were the tribal encyclopedia and could recite the history of their nation, genealogies, lists of kings, migration stories, royal political practices and etiquette, ethics, responsibilities, deities and ancestral spirits, and ceremonial sequences. They recorded techniques for hunting, smelting, blacksmithing and other critical technologies and would relate knowledge of the movement of the sun, moon and stars, cultural and social protocols, and the sequence of their complex ceremonies. All of this information was encoded on the lukasa through beads and shells.

Many Native American tribes made wampum strings and belts of white and purple beads to record treaties and other knowledge. Textiles and skins marked with a sequence of pictographic markings offer a mnemonic device, such as Lone Dog's winter count. Created by the Nakota people, each motif represents a year in the history of the tribe. The 1833 record, for example, depicts the Leonid meteor storm, while 1852 depicts the Nakota making peace with the Crow Indians.

Temporary body painting and permanent tattooing are used for ritual and mnemonic purposes by Indigenous societies across the world, including the Winnebago, Pacific Marshallese, Māori and many Malaysian tribes. Ephemeral artworks are found across most, if not all, non-text-based cultures because the process of creating an image serves to reinforce memory and the final product is of little consequence. The Native American Navajo sand painting of the earth, for example, is a memory aid for locations and animals. Each symbol represents further knowledge that is imparted through song, story or dance.

10

THE PROMISE OF SONGLINES

If Indigenous art forms are so similar and so effective in cultures around the world, why aren't we using them in contemporary Western education? Why can't we all benefit from the third archive?

The answer is simple: we can. All Indigenous knowledge techniques reflect the way the human brain stores information – the way *your* brain stores information. So why not use these knowledge methods alongside the techniques you already have? You don't have to give up writing or technology. You don't have to give up anything to add to your toolbox of memory aids and learn from the knowledge technologies that Indigenous cultures have been perfecting for millennia.

It's time to go beyond learning *about* Indigenous cultures and start learning *from* them. If you start incorporating some of the ideas in this book into your personal knowledge system, you will experience the power of Songlines.

WITHOUT MEMORY, THERE IS NO KNOWLEDGE

Almost all human knowledge is now available on the internet – you just have to search for it. So why bother memorising anything? This worrying question is asked far too often.

Firstly, you can't look up something if you don't know it exists.

Secondly, as you burrow down to specific information, you can't connect it to the bigger picture. Creativity – the way to see things in new ways and construct new ideas – depends on being able to see and understand from different directions. If you don't have various forms of knowledge in memory, how can you identify new patterns and ideas? All you are capable of doing is regurgitating the information that has already been neatly written and indexed for you.

Thirdly, how often do the knowledge keepers in every society have to make decisions based on what they know, without the time to go and look it up? How would you feel about a doctor who had to look up every symptom you mentioned? Or a policeman who had no idea what the law stated? Or a singer who knew none of the lyrics without an autocue?

Fourthly, if you want to go to the higher levels of thinking that we educators talk about endlessly in education – analyse and synthesise, hypothesise and theorise – then you have to analyse, synthesise, hypothesise or theorise about something. Otherwise, your new thinking is meaningless. By grounding your knowledge, literally, in Songlines, you have a firm knowledge base on which to build ever more complex layers of understanding.

And finally, your brain is a muscle. Like every other muscle in your body, it will slowly atrophy if you don't use it. Looking up information and regurgitating it does not exercise your brain at all.

All knowledge is based on memory, and all memory is prompted by cues. One of the great gifts on offer to us from those who understand Songlines is how to set up those cues and push our memory just that much further to a capacity we have never experienced before.

EVEN IF YOU DON'T KNOW YOUR ANCESTORS ...

It is clear from the discussion in the previous chapters that the ancestors play a very important role in conveying the knowledge encoded in the Songlines. You won't be able to instantly create the sort of relationship that Aboriginal people have with their ancestors, but you can learn from them how to enhance what you already have. You simply need to create your own set of ancestors.

Choose people from history – interesting people from a variety of subject domains. Not all of the ancestors talked about in the stories in this book were noble heroes. They were people, good and bad and complex, such as Wati Nyiru, the pursuer in the Seven Sisters Songline. The actions of complex characters enable stories to be told about the physical world, and the stories also include moral, ethical and, most importantly, emotional dimensions. The more active, dynamic and varied your characters (and, may we quietly add, the more vulgar and violent), the stronger the stories will be.

Even the most abstract and boring topic can be brought to life if you link it to a character, real or imaginary. For example, every element in the periodic table has a story behind it. Every plant and animal and law and geographic realm can be linked to someone. It doesn't have to be a person from history: you can simply use your imagination to create characters, or take them from your favourite television show or book or game. You can give voice to a pet or to that precious teddy bear in your bedroom. It won't be the same as having Aboriginal ancestors, but you will be astounded by the difference this simple method makes. Those figures can become a pantheon of characters you use across multiple domains. For example, to help you learn French, your favourite female character can engage with all the nouns in French that are feminine, and your favourite male character can engage with all the nouns that are masculine. Thinking about a particular noun will bring back the association and give you the gender. The more you let your imagination go wild, the more your characters will bring your studies to life.

Your neural networks are much more strongly laid down if you think about something and consciously engage with it. You can read an entire page from a textbook without any comprehension, but if you make the time to engage with the text by linking it to characters and stories, you can bring the information to life. Our brains love novelty. Endless repetition of the same written notes will achieve very little, but adding in stories with vibrant characters acting out information will make the notes memorable. You might struggle to come up with a story initially, but that very struggle will force your brain to engage with the information.

The chemical element boron in your imagination might become a very boring-looking person acting out the properties of the element dressed in a grey suit. The geological anticline might become a character who constantly folds rock into inverted U-shapes. Coming up with stories such as these will ensure that you don't forget the name of boron or the definition of an anticline.

Think about everything that has attracted your attention over the past week, month or year. These are the things you remember. How many of them involve people and events? How many of them require no effort to remember because you thought about the people and their stories at the time? That's what characters will do for you.

This all sounds like you are doing more work and remembering more than you had to worry about in the first place. That may be true, but your effectiveness and efficiency will be so much improved that you will find it is, in fact, less work. And more fun. The more you try it, the easier it will become.

STORIES, STORIES AND MORE STORIES

Everything in the universe that Aboriginal people can tell you about is part of a story. Humans are the only storytelling species, and from early childhood it's stories that we want to hear.

Aboriginal elders don't hide away reciting their stories to themselves in secret: they tell them to those who are ready to receive.

When they convey the knowledge, in ceremony or in private, there is always commentary and discussion. The knowledge being told is always reflected on and discussed.

One of the best ways you can learn is to teach. Explaining your knowledge to someone at a level they are ready to receive it – possibly even someone studying the same information – will show you very clearly what you do and don't understand.

There are also ceremonies based around knowledge. This sounds weird from a Western viewpoint, but if you think about it, all religions have ritualised ceremonies. Birthday parties, funerals and weddings have ritual, protocols and characters with costumes and 'acting out'. Surely our celebrations act not only to amuse but to affirm, and are quite separate from study. Why shouldn't learning be celebrated, and why shouldn't entertainment be a vessel for knowledge?

BE AT ONE WITH YOUR LANDSCAPE

Songlines are a knowledge archive perfectly tuned to the way the human brain has evolved over thousands of years. There is a reason that every Indigenous culture on the planet has engaged so intensely with their territory, their land, their home: the human brain naturally recalls information when it is triggered by physical cues in its environment. Nothing is more powerful than a location where an event has happened – you can see it clearly in your mind.

In the Indigenous worldview, all the features visible in the land were created from an ancestral event such as a battle, a place where spears were stolen, a cave where the dingo hid its family or a location where a healing ceremony occurred, leaving smoke ring patterns on the rock surface. It is at these sites of ancestral events that ceremonies relaying the whole story are performed for reinforcement and transmission. It is a dynamic learning, and the story can vary according to the context and the storyteller.

Your country, where you live, is a memory palace. It is only by experiencing your landscape in this way that you can glimpse the Indigenous connection to Country. But you can also use it to enhance your own learning. Indigenous children are taught in Country from a very young age to know the land. They learn to populate it with characters and events, building the map that will become their knowledge database.

As soon as you start encoding knowledge into any street, building, garden or area of bushland you choose, you will find that you notice details you have never noticed before. You will become aware of the sequence of houses in your street, or tree following rock in the park, or lounge room following kitchen in your house. That sequence, that Songline, offers you the most powerful memory technique ever known. It has been used for tens of thousands of years by Aboriginal people and is still used by all modern memory champions because no one has found anything better.

Every location you identify offers you a hook on which to hang information, and a cue to bring that information back to mind. Knowledge you think you have forgotten completely will return when you conjure up that location in your mind, even if you're not physically there. Your brain takes any two things it thinks of at the same time, and links them, creating a 'temporal snapshot'.

MAKE YOUR WORLD SING

In all Indigenous cultures, knowledge is performed. Think back to your childhood. Can you remember songs you learnt then? How about songs from a few years ago? Can you remember any speeches? Any rhythm, music, rhyme or repetition will make your knowledge more memorable. Music brings out an emotional response, and anything you feel emotionally is much easier to recall.

At Malmsbury Primary School in rural Victoria in 2017, a group of seventy children were taught about force. They did experiments and took notes. A week later, I asked every one of them the same two questions. First: 'Do you remember doing force in science?' They did. That put the second question in context: 'What is a force?' Three said correctly that it was a push or a pull. About half of the rest referred to things that parents made you do or friends insisted on. The rest said, 'May the force be with you!' The last option might be highly memorable, but it is not physics. The music teacher Joseph Bromley made a little song with actions to the tune of the Imperial March from *Star Wars*. The children sang it in music class and once in assembly, and then it wasn't mentioned again for over a week. Those children were then asked the same two questions about force, and every single one said or sang that a force was a push or a pull, laughing and doing the actions. Before they had learnt the song, when the first teacher was talking about force, the students were building on sand, on no firm foundation at all.[1]

You can make up songs about absolutely anything. Sometimes the natural rhythm of what you are saying will create a tune by itself, especially if you use repetition and rhyme. It is usually easier, however, to use a tune you already know. Nursery rhymes are particularly good because the melodies are so simple and easy to remember. Adding any kind of movement will make what you sing even more memorable. Thousands of years of Indigenous ceremony have proved the case.

ART IS FOR EVERYONE, EVERYWHERE AND EVERYWHEN

All cultures create art. In Indigenous cultures, everyone is an artist. In Western cultures, only some people are allowed to be artists, and this selection starts in school. In each class there are one or two recognised artists, and the other students learn that they are not artists. They might be academics or sportspeople or good at science – but no one is allowed to be seen to be good at too many things. Often if you are labelled as the arty one then you are not the brainy one or the one who has the knowledge.

This is in contradiction to the Indigenous world, where mark-making on a huge range of media – or art, as it is now called – encodes knowledge and belongs to everyone, just as books belong to everyone in the Western world. However, art has an immediacy that books do not, and art can excite an emotional response at first sighting. This encourages the visually literate to read more into a work and learn and carry that learning for as long as the image is recalled in the brain. Just like the concentration required to convert information you are studying into song, dance and story, encoding your information visually or tactually, or both, leads to a memory device that is astoundingly effective for those who have never experienced art in this way before.

Aboriginal cultures traditionally are non-text-based so designs handed down for generations are visual scripts. Any imagery makes cues stronger – even rough sketches will do. Drawings, colours, patterns, humour, drama and exaggeration all help. Designing an artwork is a concrete task that you can't do without concentrating. Thinking about how to represent the knowledge forces you to engage with it. Thinking about how to represent the relationships between all the parts forces you to concentrate more. Try to avoid using words. It only needs to act as a cue for you, not anyone else.

There are many ancient traditions, from rock art to bark painting, you can emulate – Tibetan mandalas and ancient Chinese narrative scrolls, Western art and Eastern art. There is no shortage of fantasy art telling of the past, the present, the future and other worlds. For your mnemonic art, you might want to adopt a different style from the one you usually use. Go online and search for something unique to intensify your stories and Songlines.

Don't forget the other lessons from the art that brings Songlines to life. As well as imagining characters, you can create them. While conducting research at Malmsbury Primary School with art teacher Paul Allen, I watched the students create characters using sticks and wire, wool, string and fabric, tinsel and bits of old jewellery. Paul called the resulting characters 'rapscallions'. We wanted to see how the rapscallions might help with learning across the curriculum. The students used either their own rapscallion, or small groups of rapscallions activated by their classmates, to perform science, mathematics, grammar and history stories. It was astounding to watch the students and see how naturally and vibrantly they acted out knowledge. When writing a persuasive text, having to convince someone else's rapscallion made the student's writing stronger. The students acted out stories about multiplication tables and spelling rules, the numbers associated with objects and the letters each given a personality. From there, it was easy for the students to create memorable narratives. Because they had really engaged with their personal rapscallions and those of their friends, just having the objects on the table at school brought knowledge to life through performance.

Then there are portable devices. Any decorated object can work as a memory aid. You can print or embroider images on cloth, string beads to make jewellery, or glue shells onto carved wood. You can tell stories with small objects, leaves, sticks and stones and draw in the sand.

LASTLY, MIX THEM ALL TOGETHER

Throughout this book, we have described techniques that you can adapt to bring Songlines into your own life, one at a time. The very last lesson from the Songlines is that each knowledge method is not practised in isolation from the others. As you get used to thinking this way, you will find you want to represent your Songlines in art, sing the story, talk to your characters and learn from them. You can associate your knowledge with your landscape, and you will find that you can integrate the Aboriginal techniques with those from your own experience – that is, writing and technology. You can create your personal third archive.

Songlines have been around for millennia and will be around for many millennia to come if we lend a hand to keep them alive.

11

THE LAST SONG

This may be the last chapter in this book, but it is not the end. Rather, it is the beginning of not only this series of readers on First Knowledges but your pathway to learning what they have to offer.

Like the Songlines that never end, the promise of this book is to open you up to a new way of understanding and a new way of knowing and being Australian on this continent. As an Australian you too share a kinship with the First Peoples. We are all beneficiaries of the deep history of this continent and its long human occupancy stretching back thousands of generations. Immerse yourself in this legacy. It is a shared history in a shared country.

Elders from the *Songlines* exhibition who are custodians of the Seven Sisters Songline are very clear about why all Australians need to know about the Songlines. As they say, if you want to share this country with us then you need to know your stories beyond the last couple of hundred years. If you want to truly belong to this country, as Australians, you have to know your story about this place, this continent and its creation: 'We are here to teach you your stories, not just to share ours. Without the deep stories you can't take root, you will only ever be a transplant.'

The elders are not talking about sharing their stories: they are talking about telling you your stories.

You have learnt how to discover your own Songlines that root you not only to the place and times you live in now, but to the times and place of those who came before, and those who will come after. Understanding how the Songlines work as a framework for relating people to each other and to place will give you the key to belonging. Learning how to integrate the dual knowledge systems from the first and second Australians will give you access to a third archive and with it, power over knowledge.

Songlines divulge powerful lessons about what it means to be human and to live on this earth. They offer us the promise of connectivity to each other and our planet in a fragmenting world.

ACKNOWLEDGEMENTS

Margo Neale Ngawagurrawa would like to acknowledge the community curatorium of senior custodians of the Seven Sisters Songlines exhibition: Rene Kulitja; Alison Milyika Carroll; Tapaya Edwards; Brenda, Ronnie and Stanley Douglas; Josephine Mick; Anawari Inpiti Mitchell; Jennifer Nginyaka Mitchell; Muuki Taylor; Nola Taylor; Lalla West; and in particular, Inawinytji Williamson, the spokesperson for the community curatorium. She thanks Kim Mahood, Hanson Pye, Jamie Brown, Lynette Wallworth, Mike Smith, Andrea Mason, Mathew Trinca, Sarah Kenderdine, Diana James, Christiane Keller, Sita McAlpine, the National Museum of Australia, Maruku Arts and the Tjanpi Desert Weavers. She also thanks family from the Gumbaynggirr and Kulin Nations: Robyne Bancroft and Dani Gorogo; Jirrayn, Djagali and Seremi Rawson; and Marandu, Jodi and Sonny Neale.

Lynne Kelly would like to acknowledge the Dja Dja Wurrung on whose land she lives and works. She thanks Paul Allen, Duane Hamacher, Patrick Nunn, Jennifer Rodger, Alice Steel and the staff and students of Malmsbury Primary School for their assistance. She would also like to thank her family: Damian Kelly, Sue King-Smith and Rebecca, Rudolph, Abigail and Leah Heitbaum.

The authors thank: Allen & Unwin for permission to quote from John Bradley with Yanyuwa Families, *Singing Saltwater Country: Journey to the Songlines of Carpentaria* (2010) and Gay'wu Group of Women, *Songspirals* (2019); Bloomsbury Publishing for permission to quote from Patrick Nunn, *The Edge of Memory* (2018); and the Buku-Larrnggay Mulka Centre for permission to quote from *Saltwater* (Buku-Larrngay Mulka Centre in association with Jennifer Isaacs Publishing, 1999).

IMAGE CREDITS

51   *Bandaiyan, Corpus Australis*, 1993
      David Mowaljarlai
      From David Mowaljarlai & Jutta Malnic, *Yorro Yorro:*
      Everything Standing Up Alive: Spirit of the Kimberley,
      Magabala Books, 2001.
      © the estate of David Mowaljarlai

65   Overlay diagram of *Yarrkalpa (Hunting Ground)*, 2013
      Kim Mahood
      © National Museum of Australia

77   Kuru Ala (Eyes Open), 2016
      Annieka Skinner
      © Tjanpi Desert Weavers, NPY Women's Council

154   Diagram of *Kungkarangkalpa – Seven Sisters*, 2015
      © National Museum of Australia

154   Diagram of the Anangu Pitjantjatjara Yankunytjatjara
      (APY) Seven Sisters Songline, 2017
      © National Museum of Australia

NOTES

1. PERSONAL PERSPECTIVES

1 Walter J Ong, *Orality and Literacy: The Technologizing of the Word*, Routledge, London, 1982.

2 Quoted in Ben Collins, 'How Explorer and Pirate William Dampier's Comments on Aboriginal People in 1697 Set the Tone for Future Sentiment', *ABC News*, 4 November 2018, <abc.net.au/news/2018-11-04/william-dampiers-terra-nullius-set-the-tone-for-australia/10420338>.

3 James Cook, John Hutchinson & Samuel Wallis, *Journal of HMS* Endeavour, 1768–1771, 23 August 1770, <nla.gov.au/nla.obj-229068117/view>.

4 Parliament of Australia, House of Representatives, *Debates*, Commonwealth Franchise Bill, Second Reading, 1902, p. 11,930 (Mr King O'Malley).

5 Sigmund Freud, *Totem and Taboo: Some Points of Agreement between the Mental Lives of Savages and Neurotics*, translated by James Strachey, Routledge & Kegan Paul, London, 1960, pp. 1–2. Originally *Totem und Tabu*, first published in Imago (Vienna), vol. 1–2, 1912–13.

6 Some things have not changed. There is a scene in the 2019 documentary *In My Blood It Runs* where a teacher in an Alice Springs school for Aboriginal kids is using a 1952 history textbook that tells how Captain Cook discovered Australia – a book that also contains primitivist views about Aboriginal people.

7 Margo Neale, *Yiribana: An Introduction to the Aboriginal and Torres Strait Islander Collection, the Art Gallery of New South Wales*, Art Gallery of New South Wales, Sydney, 1996, p. 128.

8 'Pioneering Australian Artist Gordon Bennett Dies at 58', *ArtAsiaPacific*, 2014, <artasiapacific.com/News/GordonBennettPioneerIndigenousAustralianArtist DiesAt58>.

9 While Aboriginal people have never been classified under a state or federal 'flora and fauna' act, it is a pervasive belief that is representative of the racism and discrimination experienced by this nation's First Peoples.

10 Lynne Kelly, *The Memory Code*, Allen & Unwin, Sydney, 2016.

2. EVERYTHING STARTS AND FINISHES WITH COUNTRY

1 Paddy Roe in Krim Benterrak, Stephen Muecke & Paddy Roe, *Reading the Country: Introduction to Nomadology*, Fremantle Arts Centre Press, Perth, 1984, p. 168.

2 'An Average Australian Bloke', *Four Corners*, ABC Television, 1996.

3 Australian Bureau of Statistics, *Aboriginal and Torres Strait Islander Population, 2016*, 2017, <abs.gov.au/ausstats/abs@.nsf/Lookup/by%20Subject/2071.0~2016~Main%20 Features~Aboriginal%20and%20Torres%20Strait%20islander%20Population%20 Article~12>.

4 Songlines Project partners and elders meeting, Amata community, South Australia, 17 April 2012.

5 Spoken at opening of *Songlines: Tracking the Seven Sisters* exhibition, National Museum of Australia, 14 September 2017.

6 Quoted in Margo Neale, 'Introduction: Alive with the Dreaming', in Margo Neale (ed.), *Songlines: Tracking the Seven Sisters*, National Museum of Australia Press, Canberra, 2017, p. 15.

7 See Diana Young's essay 'On Revealing and Concealing', in Neale (ed.), p. 72.

8 Mike Smith, 'The Metaphysics of Songlines', in Neale (ed.), p. 219.

9 Deborah Bird Rose coined the term 'wounded spaces' in her book *Reports from a Wild Country: Ethics for Decolonisation*, University of New South Wales Press, Sydney, 2004, p. 34.

10 John Bradley with Yanyuwa Families, *Singing Saltwater Country: Journey to the Songlines of Carpentaria*, Allen & Unwin, Sydney, 2010.

3. KNOWLEDGE IN COUNTRY AND THE THIRD ARCHIVE

1 Inuit elder Dempsey Bob, speaking at the opening of *People of the Cedar: First Nations Art from the Northwest Coast of Canada* exhibition at National Museum of Australia, Canberra, 2 March 2006.

2 Fred Myers, *Pintupi Country, Pintupi Self: Sentiment, Place, and Politics among Western Desert Aborigines*, Smithsonian Institution Press, Washington, DC; Australian Institute of Aboriginal Studies, Canberra, 1986, p. 53.

3 In John Carty et al., *We Don't Need a Map: A Martu Experience of the Western Desert*, Fremantle Arts Centre, Fremantle, WA, 2013, p. 41.

4 Darren Jorgensen & Ian McLean (eds), *Indigenous Archives: The Making and Unmaking of Aboriginal Art*, UWA Publishing, Perth, 2017.

5 Jorgensen & McLean.

6 Bruce Chatwin, *The Songlines*, Jonathan Cape, London, 1987.

7 Carty et al., p. 40.

8 Carty et al., p. 40.

9 Sydney gallerist Christopher Hodges talks about this in the film *Emily in Japan: The Making of an Exhibition*, Ronin Films, 2009.

10 David Miller, chairman of Ananguku Arts and Cultural Aboriginal Corporation, at a meeting of Songlines elders and partners at Australian National University in Canberra, 2010.

11 Quoted in *Djalkiri: We Are Standing on Their Names, Blue Mud Bay*, Nomad Art Productions, Parap, NT, 2010, p. 22.

12 *Djalkiri*, p. 22.

13 Alan Rumsey, 'The Dreaming, Human Agency and Inscriptive Practice', *Oceania*, 65(2), 1994, pp. 116–30.

14 Painting on canvas derives from body painting: the black undercoat represents black skin.

15 Lynette Wallworth, 'Always Walking Country', in Margo Neale (ed.), *Songlines: Tracking the Seven Sisters*, National Museum of Australia Press, Canberra, 2017, p. 48.
16 Kim Mahood, 'The Seething Landscape', in Neale (ed), p. 35.

4. SONGLINES TODAY

1 *Ngurru Kuju Walyja: Canning Stock Route Project*, <canningstockrouteproject.com>.
2 William L Fox, 'Thinking about Painting', in Steve Morton, Mandy Martin, Kim Mahood & John Carty (eds), *Desert Lake: Art, Science and Stories from Paruku*, CSIRO Publishing, Melbourne, 2013, p. 230.
3 Fox, p. 230.
4 Fox, pp. 229–30.
5 The original story of the male and female dingoes is well established and often told, as is the story of the two brothers who intersect with the dingoes before becoming the two hills, so this is an active reinterpretation by Hanson Pye of two known stories. This telling occurred at the Araluen Arts Centre in Alice Springs in 2013 and was recounted to the author by Kim Mahood in Canberra in 2015.
6 Details of the story of Seven Sisters vary across time and between language group and storyteller, with differences occurring in both the actions of the characters and the nature of the event. Sometimes it is the eldest sister who was harmed by Wati Nyiru; other times, it is multiple sisters who suffered at the hands of their pursuer. What remains consistent, though, is the focus on unwanted male attention and the sisters' strength in unity as they flee across the country.
7 Quoted in Margo Neale, 'White Man Got No Dreaming', in Margo Neale (ed.), *Songlines: Tracking the Seven Sisters*, National Museum of Australia Press, Canberra, 2017, p. 206.

5. SONGLINES AND SYNAPSES

1 John Bradley with Yanyuwa Families, *Singing Saltwater Country: Journey to the Songlines of Carpentaria*, Allen & Unwin, Sydney, 2010, p. 41.
2 Bradley with Yanyuwa Families, p. 29.
3 Cliff Goddard & Arpad Kalotas (comps & eds), *Punu: Yankunytjatjara Plant Use – Traditional Methods of Preparing Foods, Medicines, Utensils and Weapons from Native Plants*, Angus & Robertson, Sydney, 2002, p. iv.
4 Robert MW Dixon & Grace Koch, *Dyirbal Song Poetry: The Oral Literature of an Australian Rainforest People*, University of Queensland Press, Brisbane, 1996.
5 Peter R Schmidt, *Historical Archaeology in Africa: Representation, Social Memory, and Oral Traditions*, AltaMira Press, Lanham, Maryland, 2006, pp. 139–52.
6 Lynne Kelly, *Knowledge and Power in Prehistoric Societies: Orality, Memory and the Transmission of Culture*, Cambridge University Press, New York, 2015, pp. 250–1.

7   Catherine J Ellis & Linda Barwick, 'Antikirinja Women's Song Knowledge 1963–72: Its Significance in Antikirinja Culture', in Peggy Brock (ed.), *Women, Rites and Sites: Aboriginal Women's Cultural Knowledge*, Allen & Unwin, Sydney, 1989, p. 26.

8   Dominic O'Brien, *Learn to Remember: Practical Techniques and Exercises to Improve Your Memory*, Chronicle Books, San Francisco, 2000.

6. SONGLINES SPIRAL FOREVER

1   Gay'wu Group of Women, *Songspirals*, Allen & Unwin, Sydney, 2019, pp. xvi, xvii.

2   Stanner coined the term 'everywhen' in his 1956 essay 'The Dreaming'.

3   See Howard Morphy's books *Aboriginal Art* (Phaidon Press, London, 1998) and *Ancestral Connections* (University of Chicago Press, Chicago, 1991).

4   Bill Gammage, *The Biggest Estate on Earth: How Aborigines Made Australia*, Allen & Unwin, Sydney, 2012; Bruce Pascoe, *Dark Emu: Aboriginal Australia and the Birth of Agriculture*, Magabala Books, Broome, 2018.

5   Parks Australia, 'Anangu culture', n.d., <parksaustralia.gov.au/uluru/discover/culture/>.

6   Patrick Nunn, *The Edge of Memory*, Bloomsbury Sigma, London, 2018.

7   Nunn, pp. 129, 131.

8   Quoted in Dale Kerwin, *Aboriginal Dreaming Paths and Trading Routes*, Sussex Academic Press, Brighton, 2010, pp. 48–9.

9   Catherine J Ellis & Linda Barwick, 'Antikirinja Women's Song Knowledge 1963–72: Its Significance in Antikirinja Culture', in Peggy Brock (ed.), *Women, Rites and Sites: Aboriginal Women's Cultural Knowledge*, Allen & Unwin, Sydney, 1989, p. 30.

10   Kerwin, p. 47.

11   Kerwin, p. 40.

12   John Bradley with Yanyuwa Families, *Singing Saltwater Country: Journey to the Songlines of Carpentaria*, Allen & Unwin, Sydney, 2010, p. 37.

7. SONGLINES EMBRACE THE GLOBE

1   Like many Western terms for Indigenous cultural roles, 'medicine man' is confusing for those unfamiliar with Native American cultures. The term is often used by Native American elders when identifying themselves, as here. In specific medicine societies, the 'medicine men' and women are the knowledge experts. There are also many other knowledge roles within Native American society.

2   Keith H Basso, *Wisdom Sits in Places*, University of New Mexico Press, Albuquerque, 1996.

3   Basso, pp. 45–6.

4   Kurt F Anschuetz, 'A Healing Place: Rio Grande Pueblo Cultural Landscapes and the Petroglyph National Monument', in KF Anschuetz et al., *'That Place People Talk About': The Petroglyph National Monument Ethnographic Landscape Report*,

unpublished manuscript, on file with National Park Service, Petroglyph National Monument, 2002, p. 3.33.

5   David Cranz, 1767, quoted in John MacDonald, *The Arctic Sky: Inuit Astronomy, Star Lore, and Legend*, Royal Ontario Museum/Nunavut Research Institute, Toronto, 1998, p. 2.

6   John Bennett & Susan Rowley (comps & eds), *Uqalurait: An Oral History of Nunavut*, McGill-Queen's University Press, Montreal, 2004, p. 120.

7   MacDonald, p. 168.

8   Dominique Tungilik, Arviligjuarmiut, 1976, quoted in Bennett & Rowley (comps & eds), *Uqalurait: An Oral History of Nunavut*, p. 113.

9   MacDonald, pp. 174, 177.

8. SONGLINES IN SEA AND SKY

1   Gay'wu Group of Women, *Songspirals*, Allen & Unwin, Sydney, 2019, p. 12.

2   Gay'wu Group of Women, p. 47.

3   Gay'wu Group of Women, p. 20.

4   Gay'wu Group of Women, p. 30.

5   Patrick Nunn, *The Edge of Memory*, Bloomsbury Sigma, London, 2018, pp. 184–5.

6   Duane W Hamacher, John Barsa, Segar Passi & Alo Tapim, 'Indigenous Use of Stellar Scintillation to Predict Weather and Seasonal Change', *Proceedings of the Royal Society of Victoria*, 131, 2019, pp. 24–33 (p. 24).

7   Hamacher et al., pp. 26–7.

8   Quoted in Duane W Hamacher, *A Framework for Exploring Indigenous Astronomical Knowledge in the Torres Strait*, Monash Indigenous Centre, Monash University, Melbourne, 2019, p. 7.

9   Gay'wu Group of Women, pp. 131–2.

10 Robert S Fuller, Michael G Anderson, Ray P Norris & Michelle Trudgett, 'The Emu Sky Knowledge of the Kamilaroi and Euahlayi Peoples', *Journal of Astronomical History and Heritage*, 17(2), 2014, pp. 171–9.

11 Ray P Norris & Bill Yidumduma Harney, 'Songlines and Navigation in Wardaman and other Australian Aboriginal Cultures', *Journal of Astronomical History and Heritage*, 17(2), 2014, pp. 141–8 (pp. 143–4).

12 Norris & Harney, pp. 145, 146–7.

13 Roslynn D Haynes, 'Astronomy and the Dreaming: The Astronomy of the Aboriginal Australians', in Helaine Selin (ed.), *Astronomy Across Cultures: The History of Non-Western Astronomy*, Kluwer Academic Publishers, Dordrecht, 2000, p. 68.

14 Quoted in *Ngurra Kuju Walya: One Country One People – Stories from the Canning Stock Route*, Macmillan Art Publishing, Melbourne, 2011, p. 34.

9. ART IS CULTURE MADE VISIBLE

1   Margo Neale (ed.), *Songlines: Tracking the Seven Sisters*, National Museum of Australia Press, Canberra, 2017, p. 92.

2   Spoken at opening of *Songlines: Tracking the Seven Sisters* exhibition, National Museum of Australia, 14 September 2017.

3   Buku-Larrnggay Mulka Centre, *Saltwater: Yirrkala Bark Paintings of Sea Country*, Buku-Larrnggay Mulka Centre in association with Jennifer Isaacs Publishing, Sydney, 1999, p. 20.

4   Dale Kerwin, *Aboriginal Dreaming Paths and Trading Routes*, Sussex Academic Press, Brighton, 2010, p. 13.

5   Neale (ed.), p. 48.

6   Howard Morphy, *Aboriginal Art*, Phaidon Press, London, 1998, p. 51.

7   Morphy, p. 183.

8   Museum Victoria, *Bunjilaka: The Aboriginal Centre at Melbourne Museum*, Museum Victoria, Melbourne, 2000, p. 34.

9   Museum Victoria, p. 34

10 Nungarrayi, personal communication, 2010.

11 Buku-Larrnggay Mulka Centre, p. 10.

12 Buku-Larrnggay Mulka Centre, p. 6.

10. THE PROMISE OF SONGLINES

1   Research conducted by Lynne Kelly at Malmsbury Primary School in 2017.

FURTHER READING

Basso, Keith H, *Wisdom Sits in Places: Landscape and Language among the Western Apache*, University of New Mexico Press, Albuquerque, 1996.

Buku-Larrnggay Mulka Centre, *Saltwater: Yirrkala Bark Paintings of Sea Country – Recognising Indigenous Sea Rights*, Buku-Larrnggay Mulka Centre in association with Jennifer Isaacs Publishing, Sydney, 1999.

Gay'wu Group of Women, *Songspirals: Sharing Women's Wisdom of Country Through Songlines*, Allen & Unwin, Sydney, 2019.

Gilchrist, Stephen (ed.), *Everywhen: The Eternal Presence in Indigenous Art from Australia*, Harvard Art Museums, Cambridge, Mass., 2016.

Kelly, Lynne, *Knowledge and Power in Prehistoric Societies: Orality, Memory and the Transmission of Culture*, Cambridge University Press, New York, 2015.

—— *The Memory Code*, Allen & Unwin, Sydney, NSW, 2016.

—— *Memory Craft*, Allen & Unwin, Sydney, 2019.

Kerwin, Dale, *Aboriginal Dreaming Paths and Trading Routes: The Colonisation of the Australian Economic Landscape*, Sussex Academic Press, Brighton, 2010.

Kleinert, Sylvia & Margo Neale (eds), *The Oxford Companion to Aboriginal Art and Culture*, Oxford University Press, Melbourne, 2000.

Morphy, Howard, *Ancestral Connections: Art and an Aboriginal System of Knowledge*, University of Chicago Press, Chicago, 1991.

—— *Aboriginal Art*, Phaidon Press, London, 1998.

Neale, Margo, *Emily Kame Kngwarreye: Alhalkere – Paintings from Utopia*, Queensland Art Gallery, Brisbane, & Macmillan, Melbourne, 1998.

—— *Urban Dingo: The Art of Lin Onus, 1948–1996*, Craftsman House in association with Queensland Art Gallery, Sydney, 2000.

—— 'The Presentation and Interpretation of Aboriginal and Torres Strait Islander Art: The Yiribana Gallery in Focus', in Michele Grossman (ed.), *Blacklines: Contemporary Critical Writings by Indigenous Australians*, Melbourne University Publishing, Melbourne, 2003, pp. 104–8.

—— 'The Politics of Visibility: How Indigenous Australian Art Found Its Way into Art Galleries', in Caroline Turner (ed.), *Art and Social Change: Contemporary Art in Asia and the Pacific*, Pandanus Books, Research School of Pacific and Asian Studies, Australian National University, Canberra, 2005, pp. 483–97.

—— 'God Lives in the Dreaming: Aboriginal Treasures in the Vatican', *Artlink Indigenous: Beauty and Terror*, Artlink Australia, Adelaide, 31(2), 2011.

Neale, Margo (ed.), *Utopia: The Genius of Emily Kame Kngwarreye*, National Museum of Australia Press, Canberra, 2008.

—— *Songlines: Tracking the Seven Sisters*, National Museum of Australia Press, Canberra, 2017.

Neale, Margo & Ann Jackson-Nakano, *Introduction to Aboriginal and Torres Strait Islander Art*, Barrie Publishing, Melbourne, 2003.

Neale, Margo & Martin Thomas (eds), *Exploring the Legacy of the 1948 Arnhem Land Expedition*, ANU E Press, Australian National University, Canberra, 2011.

Nunn, Patrick, *The Edge of Memory: Ancient Stories, Oral Tradition and the Post-Glacial World*, Bloomsbury Sigma, London, 2018.

Rose, Deborah Bird, *Dingo Makes Us Human: Life and Land in an Aboriginal Australian Culture*, Cambridge University Press, Cambridge & Melbourne, 1992.

INDEX

The best of both worlds

TITLES IN THE
FIRST KNOWLEDGES SERIES

SONGLINES
Margo Neale & Lynne Kelly
(2020)

DESIGN
Alison Page & Paul Memmott
(2021)

COUNTRY
Bill Gammage & Bruce Pascoe
(2021)

MEDICINE & PLANTS
(2022)

ASTRONOMY
(2022)

INNOVATION
(2023)

Published in conjunction with the National Museum of Australia
and supported by the Australia Council for the Arts.